THE COLLECTED EDITION OF *UFO-mation*

Published Quaterly by NYSIB: The New York Saucer Information Bureau

John Hay

SAUCERIAN PUBLISHER

ISBN:978-1-7366564-1-9
ISBN-13:978-1-7366564-1-9
GTIN-14:09781736656419
•
© 2022, Saucerian Publisher

Al rights reserved. No part of this publication maybe reproduced, translate, distribute, store in a retrieval system, or transmitted in any form or by any means, electronic, mechanical, photocopying, recording or otherwise, without prior written permision from the publisher.

Prologue

It is generally a good idea to return to the classics in any genre. This also goes for UFO literature. Rereading a book after ten or twenty years is a rewarding experience. You will discover new data and ideas you didn´t notice before. The reason, of course, is that you are, in many ways, not the same person reading the book the second or third time. Hopefully, you have advanced in knowledge, experience, intellectual and spiritual discernment. A good starting point is to reread the UFO classics of the 1960s, in order to understand the deeper mystery involved in what happened during that era.

UFO-mation was a saucer mimeographed newsletter published by John Hay, as Editor, and Bruce Dolen as Co-editor, from New York, New York, under the banner of the New York Saucer Information Bureau. The main idea behind *UFO-mation*, like many similar publications of that time, was to create a forum for UFO experience and saucer sightings for the purpose of the investigation of spacecraft, extra-terrestrial travel, and other subjects relating to these matters in order to encourage public support of projects in connection with these phenomena.

Saucerian Publisher was founded with the mission of promoting books in Ufology, Paranormal, and the Occult. Our vision is to preserve the legacy of literary history by reprint editions of books which have already been exhausted or are difficult to obtain. Our goal is to help readers, educators and researchers by bringing back original publications that are difficult to find at reasonable price, while preserving the legacy of universal knowledge. Very rare *UFO-mation ,edition!* This is a rare set of *UFO-mation* issues published by New York Saucer Information Bureau, between 1958- 59. These are VERY hard to come across these days. We decided to published them as a collected edition as a set to make it easier for someone to add them to their flying saucer / UFO collection. This title is an authentic reproduction of the original printed text in shades of gray. **THIS IS NOT A COMPLETED COLLECTIONS. SOME ISSUES ARE MISSING. IMPORTANT:** Despite the fact that we have attempted to accurately maintain the integrity of the original work, the present reproduction may have minor errors beyond our control like: missing and blurred pages, poor pictures and readers' pencil markings from the original scanned copy. **HOWEVER**, because this book is culturally important, we have made available as part of our commitment to protect, preserve and promote knowledge in the world. These issues are an authentic reproduction of the issues of the *UFO-mation* for the years: 1958-1959. Great, but unpretentious, these issues are extraordinarily rare symbols by themselves of what was going on in those early years of the modern UFO era. This collected edition has the following issues of *UFO-mation* : Vol. I--#3 (May 7th, April 15 th, April 21 st, 1958); Vol 1 No 1 (Winter Issue); Vol 1, No 2 (Spring Issue); Vol 1 No 3 (Summer Issue); Vol 1 No 4 (Fall Issue, 1959).

Editor
Saucerian Publisher, 2022

UFO-mation

Published Quarterly by NYSIB: The New York Saucer Information Bureau

VOL. I--#3.   MAY 7th 1958

25 Cents

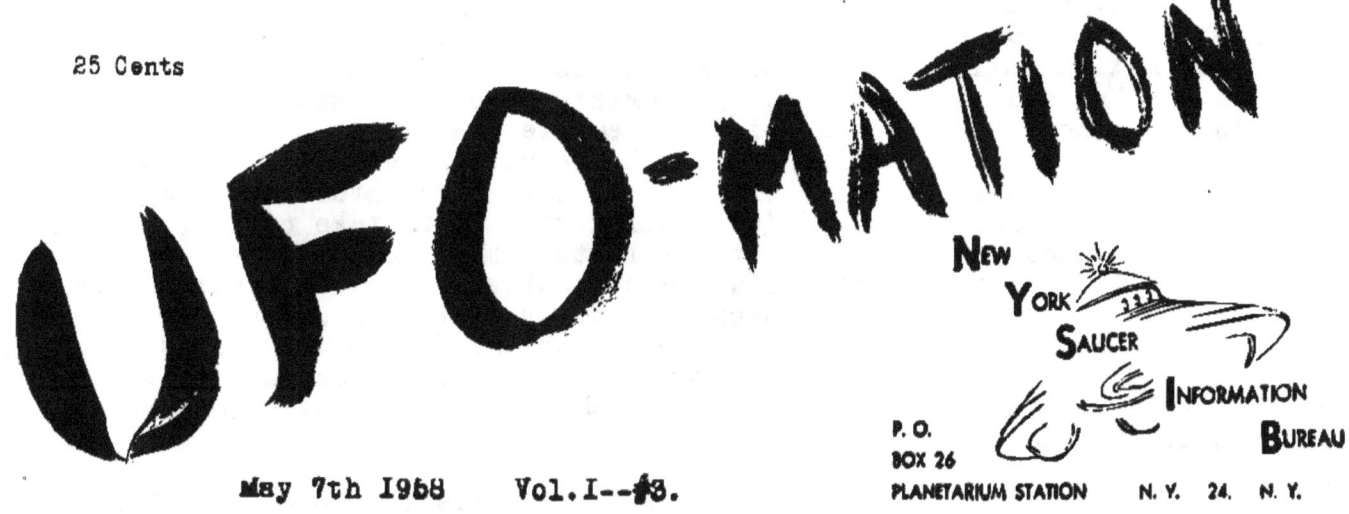

UFO-MATION

New York Saucer Information Bureau

May 7th 1958 Vol.I--#3.

P. O. BOX 26
PLANETARIUM STATION   N.Y. 24. N.Y.

Enclosed in this issue are copies of letters sent to President Eisenhower and the Federal Tax Dept. If you agree with the principles of these two letters, you can help bring about an effective change in the nuclear situation and also get a break-through in the Flying Saucer Mystery, by writing similar letters to the President and your local tax Director. If the peoples of the world want war, they will get war. It is their money and your money that turns the wheels of all war machinery. Stop it from the source and there will be no machines to wage war. Then and only then, will people be able to live in peace and harmony on this planet and gain the right to venture into Outer Space. God help the Universe if MAN (from Earth) is allowed to spread the rotten apple of his present hates among the baskets of plenty in the Cosmos.

NYSIB wants to apologize to the New Jersey Residents on our mailing list for the inexcusable way that the P.O. sent our cards out BULK MAIL, when they were mailed FIRST CLASS. This time it was the Palisades Park P.O. We have demanded a refund, and a letter from the Post Master, "regretting" the occurrence, says the matter has been brought to the attention of the District Manager. Write to this P.O. and add your complaint to ours if you want to receive your cards in time for lectures. We can only do so much.

If you want a close-up on the Brazilian UFO high-lights, send to J.Escobar Faria, Rua 13 de Maio, No. 1240, Sao Paulo, Brazil, for his UFO-CRITICAL BULLETIN. An abundance of ufomation, right up to date, including the now famous Trinidad sighting and pictures taken from a Brazilian Naval Research Vessel. It is a free publication, but don't take advantage of this fact. Send a contribution and money for stamps. Specify AIR MAIL if you want it fast, the overland route takes almost a month. $1:00 will cover airmail for about three issues.

Musts for your UFO library----Max B. Miller's "FLYING SAUCERS-FACT OR FICTION", loaded with pictures and info. 75cts. Ray Palmer's May issue and future ones of "FLYING SAUCERS FROM OTHER WORLDS", featuring among other fine articles, Kenneth Arnold's out of print "THE COMING OF THE SAUCERS" and an excellent play-by-play account of LONG JOHN NEBEL'S WOR "PARTY LINE", by Augie Roberts and Dominick Lucchesi, entitled "SAUCERS IN THE WEE HOURS". The new issue of"UFOLOGER" ed. and pub. by Jim Villard and Dan Washburn is a whopper and a credit to these two fine young men. Gray Barker's "SAUCERIAN BULLETIN" has a personal interview with OTIS T. CARR, the gentleman claiming discovery of the source of free energy. The LITTLE LISTENING POST, fresh and stimulating as ever.

The NYSIB members who attended the last bi-monthly meeting sent a wire to Rep. CHET HOLIFIELD, House of Representatives, urging passage of Senate bill #3474 and H.of R. bill #11426. These bills are against the arming of of other Allied Nations with Nuclear Weapons. It is enough that the U.S., Russia and England have polluted the Earth's atmosphere with uncontrollable atomic radiation. When is man going to realize that he is paying through the nose so that he may eventually smell the putrification of his own body? LLOYD ANDERSON, Asst. Director of NYSIB is now in the process of setting up the NYSIB LECTURE BUREAU. It's function will be to take care of all the paper and advance work necessary for a lecture tour contemplated by any individual interested in the Flying Saucer Subject. The big hindrance to lecture tours in the past, has been the outlay of time and money by potential lecturers that could ill-afford both; the NYSIB LECTURE BUREAU will alleviate this obstacle. All F.S. organizations interested in participating in this effort, please contact LLOYD ANDERSON and he will send you all pertinent information.

From Wash. D.C. April 25th. INS RELEASE. Three distinguished scientists, Dr. Furnas, Chancellor of the U.of Buffalo, Dr.DuBridge, President of the Cal. Institute of Technology and Dr.Pickering, Director of the Jet Propulsion Laboratory, warned Congress against letting the armed services dominate Space Research, or spend vast sums of money for such "useless projects" as a weapons base on the moon. They urged CIVILIAN CONTROL of space programs. NYSIB is in full agreement with the three doctors.

Why hasn't one single scientist in this country been able to even give a theory as to how the Russians put 1000 LBS into orbit? We're having trouble trying to get 22 lbs up there. Maybe OTIS T. CARR is right, maybe the Russians have already dispensed with rockets and have an ANTI-GRAVITY device that works.

NYSIB mail brings in additional sightings every week, that people have never talked about because of ridicule, and once in a while we get a contact story. We have two very exciting contact stories from professional people that are both important members of their communities. Unfortunately because of their positions they want no publicity. These people have been kind enough afterfrequent letters to me, to write me their experiences. Anyone who has had an experience, put it down on paper, as detailed as possible and send it to NYSIB. There is only one key to our P.O.Box, and I am the only person who opens the letters, so if you prefer to remain unpublicised, at least let us have your experience on file, so that when the official secrecy lifts, and ridicule will not be the order of the day, we may openly add your name to the lists of those fortunate enough to have made contact. It will make an impressive list for the skeptics.

A space message CHAIN-LETTER starting to circulate in the N.Y.--N.J. area regardless of where it comes from, is a worthwhile project for anyone with fifteen minutes to spare. If you get one, pass it along, it can't do any harm, and it could do a tremendous amount of good.

Only one of our members that we know of is going to the Giant Rock Convention this year. George Van Tassel should be prepared for a tremendous crowd and we all hope that the convention won't be dampened by bad weather this time.

HARRY STURDEVANT, the night-watchman who had an experience with a UFO while on the job, finally got his Workman's Compensation case brought to trial but with unfortunate results. His claim was disallowed, the judge deciding that what he saw was an hallucination. STURDEVANT has until May 20th to appeal and NYSIB is doing what it can to get a lawyer interested in the case, one who will see to it that STURDEVANT gets a fair trial, which, from the looks of things, after investigating the case, does not seem to be the case in this last one, especially after the Referee at his Hearing, over a year ago, <u>decided in STURDEVANT'S favor</u>, stating that the Workman's Compensation Board was not interested in whether or not STURDEVANT saw a Flying Saucer, only whether or not he was taken sick on the job. His (the referee's) decision showed he was satisfied with the evidence that STURDEVANT <u>was</u> taken sick on the job. Now we have another line of professional people setting themselves up as authorities on UFOs--JUDGES; and in this case, at least according to the various newspaper accounts, the verdict was reached, all cut and dried--- HALLUCINATION! Was this <u>justice</u> or <u>prejudice</u>? Apparently the fact that STURDEVANT hadn't been able to work for a year and a half, was adjudged sick on the job by the Referee and according to him (Sturdevant), now, still having throat convulsions daily from the effects of the unknown forces that penetrated his lungs, seemed to have no bearing on the case. NYSIB is furthering it's investigation into this case and invites any Lawyer that would be interested, to get in touch as soon as possible. Failing an appeal in time, which costs money that STURDEVANT does not have, anyone that knows of the prospect of a job for this gentleman, can contact NYSIB with the information and get his address. This is the least we can do for a person who has been through what he has regardless whether or not you believe his story.

We have had so many requests for the pamphlet we gave out at REINHOLD O. SCHMIDT's lecture last month, with the sketch of the cigar shaped craft he boarded in Kearney, Neb, last Nov. 5th and in which he subsequently took a ride last Feb. we herewith print a facsimile of it, exactly as given to us. Bear in mind that this is an artist's conception of what SCHMIDT told him he saw.

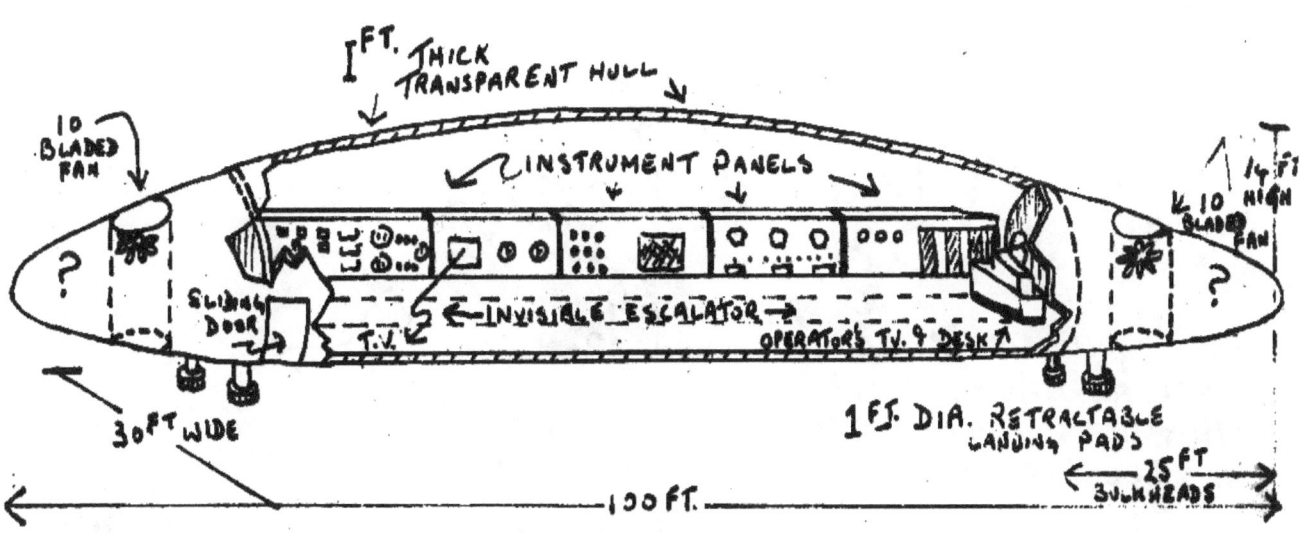

An NBC Radio news item on the 30th of May, stated that a reporter had been to 10 of the leading cities including N.Y. and Chicago and <u>not found the slightest signs of recession</u> in any of them. Does this mean that we are being handed a line from our Government? Just because a few big car and appliance manufacturers overstocked and blundered badly in their thinking that the American would continue to fall for the "better-than-ever" new model every year pitch, that has finally reached the saturation point. In a conversation with one New York Bank official, this reporter was told that <u>more</u> people are saving <u>more</u> money than ever before. This isn't consistent with what is printed in the newspapers and given out over T.V. and radio these days. Let's not be lead by the nose to another '29 slaughter.

Those who have seen or own the beautiful brochure mailed out by OTC ENTERPRISES, should be very interested to compare his artist's conception of the Flying Foil he claims to be able to build for $20 million with the very recent Brazilian Navy picture of a UFO taken over Trinidad. Below is a sketch of the Teletype picture received in the U.S. which was so obviously withheld from national coverage. When NYSIB receives copies from Brazil of the <u>four</u> pictures taken, they will be given special treatment in "UFOMATION".

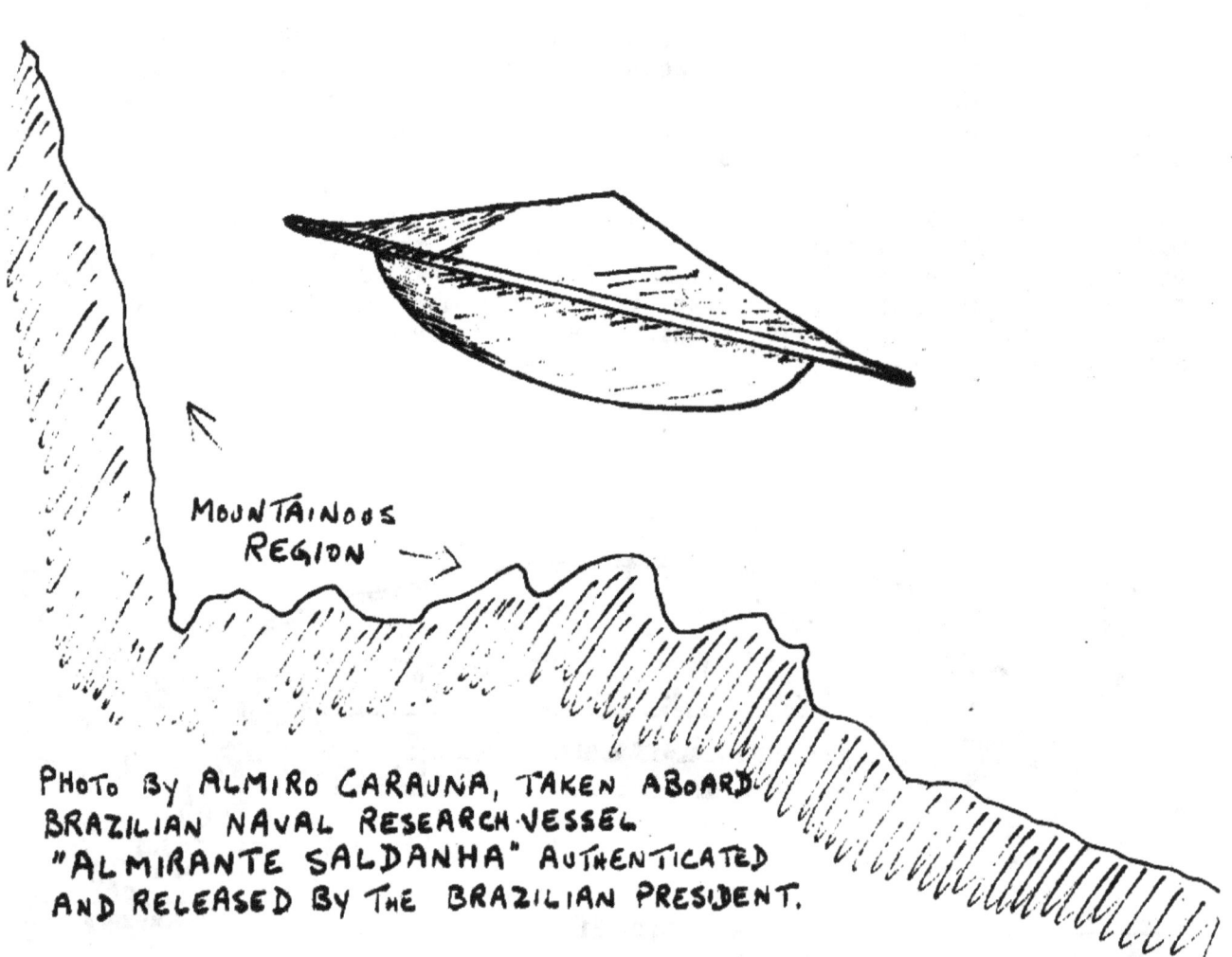

MOUNTAINOUS REGION →

PHOTO BY ALMIRO CARAUNA, TAKEN ABOARD BRAZILIAN NAVAL RESEARCH VESSEL "ALMIRANTE SALDANHA" AUTHENTICATED AND RELEASED BY THE BRAZILIAN PRESIDENT.

Quote from N.Y. TIMES, Nov 6th 1957, in the words of GENERAL OMAR N. BRADLEY. "Missiles will bring anti-missiles, and anti-missiles will bring anti-anti-missiles. But inevitably this whole electronic house of cards will reach a point where it can be constructed no higher.....When that time comes there will be nothing we can do other than to settle down uneasily..... in the thickening shadow of death...how long--would I ask you---can we put off salvation? When does humanity run out?

UFO-mation

Published Quarterly by NYSIB: The New York Saucer Information Bureau

VOL. I--#3. APRIL 15Th 1958

COPY

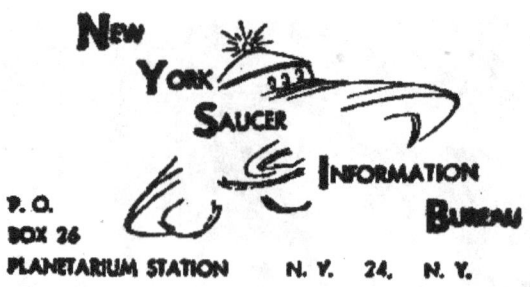

P.O. BOX 26
PLANETARIUM STATION   N.Y. 24, N.Y.

April 15th 1958

Office of the District Director
U.S. Treasury
Internal Revenue Dept
484 Lexington Ave
N.Y.C.

Dear Sir,
     Enclosed is my income tax return for 1957. $250x55 was taken out of my salaries last year for Federal Withholding Tax. I presumably owe additional money.

     As Director of the above organization, which has been in operation since Jan Ist 1958, I have come to the very definite conclusion,(and I'm by no means alone in this matter,with names of many in scientific, political and professional circles at my disposal,) that our Government with the U.S. Air Force, is holding back information of tremendous import from the American people. Our Government is not alone is this matter. We have had a committee at work at the U.N. and have already covered over 50 different Countries' Delegates. They all say the same thing. Their Governments will not allow them to make any statements. Mighty strange for something that our own (and other countries) Air Force is spending millions of dollars on, and yet keeps saying doesn't exist! Our organization, along with the hundreds of others like it all over the country is going to try and get a break-through on this vitally important subject just as soon as possible. All over the world right now, people are banding together to try and stop this insane "atomic age" that we have been pushed into without even being asked. Who knows what our children and their's will have to contend with, because a few people decided to go crazy. As far as I personally am concerned, I want no part of this devil's inferno that is being hastened to completion. I have always paid my taxes, not fully realizing what the money was going for, but there's something I can't buy with money, an easy conscience, and now that I'm fully aware of the enormity of this crime that we are all a part of, that of arming ourselves for total destruction the world over, I want it put on record that far from evading income taxes, above the normal amounts, which are very necessary, I cannot see myself adding to something that has over-reached the bounds of reason. We say on T.V. and Radio that we are a God-fearing nation. This is hypocracy in the ultimate form. We are not God-fearing, we openly acknowledge that He doesn't exist, in our every word and action during every day. If we were God-fearing and God-loving, we would automatically realize we don't need hydrogen bombs to vanquish our enemies. Maybe this all sounds like a lot of religious gibberish but as I stood in-side Jefferson's monument only two weeks ago and read some of the words engraved on the walls, I can just see that great man shaking his head in bewilderment at the way we speak his inspired words, then quite unconcernedly, even smugly, act as if we'd never heard of the Constitution, of Civil Rights and the Pursuit of Happiness. As a citizen of the U.S. I have the right above all else to freedom of Religion, and the God I worship makes no compromise for killing and war. If I have to choose sides, I'll take His side, any time. I have nothing to hide about my taxes, I've been called in the last three years, owe a few dollars on recently made additional taxes, because someone has to pay the tremendous cost of all the additional help that mounts every year as we become a nation of statistics and red tape. This could be the reason that the truth about Flying Saucers is being withheld from the public. Wash. D.C. has become a highly inefficient paper mill, with "top secret" stamped on everything from a well-known scientist's new type of target bow to a white collar worker's bill of sale for a gross of pencils in the Dept. of Defense. (Both facts, incidentally, as related over N.B.C. News recently). I'm perfectly willing to go to court any time I'm called, we've been trying to get the Civil Liberties Union to take the case of one Reinhold O. Schmidt, who was held in jail in Kearney, Neb. for three days without a warrant, then contrary to his rights as a Citizen committed to the State Mental Institution without any kind of due process of the law. All because he had told the Sheriff and Police Cheif that he had had an experience with a U.F.O. I have seen a lot of the photostated, documented evidence, and if the F.B.I. and the Air Force are allowed to get away with what they are doing, there's no knowing where this may lead us. The lawyer we talked to in the Civil Liberties Union, said the case scared him too much and he wouldn't touch it with a ten foot pole. Schmidt's is by no means the first case that we know about, it has been happening all over the country. Why? We have repeated quotes from the Air Force that Flying Saucers do not involve the security of the country, then they turn around and say they don't exist, calling a lot of our best Air Line pilots a bunch of liars, incompetents etc., these men, who have the responsibility of thousnads of lives in their hands every year. So far, regardless of the Air Force slanders, it's interesting to note that not one of these pilots has ever been fired for having had sightings. If you yourself, Sir, are interested in knowing more about what is going on, I suggest you attend our next lecture at the Palm Gardens Ballroom, 306 West 52nd St. N.Y.C. at 8:00 pm on May 8th 1958. Our guest speaker is the noted news commentator, Frank Edwards, who was fired from the A.B.C. Radio network for talking too much about Flying Saucers. You will undoubtedly find out that there are an awful lot of people who feel the same way I do. There's not much I can do about the money withheld from salaries I receive, even though I am against it, but anything additional I have something to say about.

Our Government is supposedly of the people and by the people, and as one of the people I am taking this opportunity to voice my discontent at the way it is being run, in an effort to help stop the insane rush toward global suicide. Money is the madness that man has made his idol; without it to spend so freely, maybe the idol will lose face and crawl off it's man-made pedestal.

Sincerely

Douglas Deane

UFO-mation

Published Quarterly by NYSIB: The New York Saucer Information Bureau

VOL. I--#3. APRIL 21 St 1958

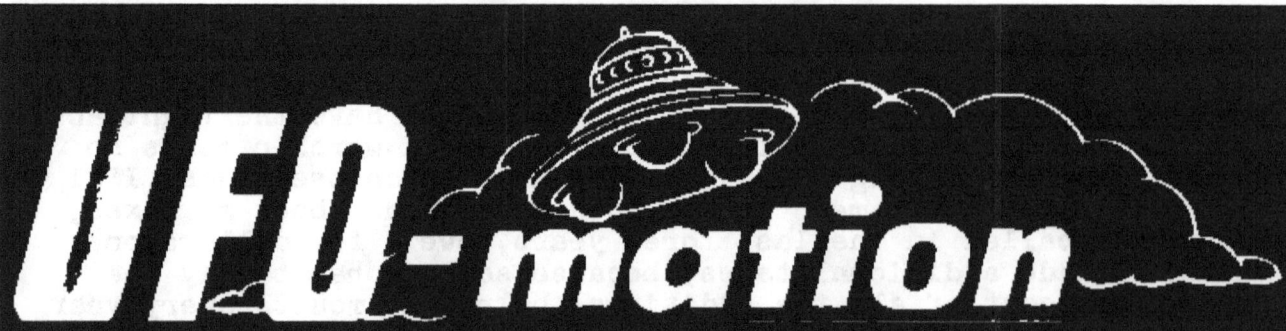

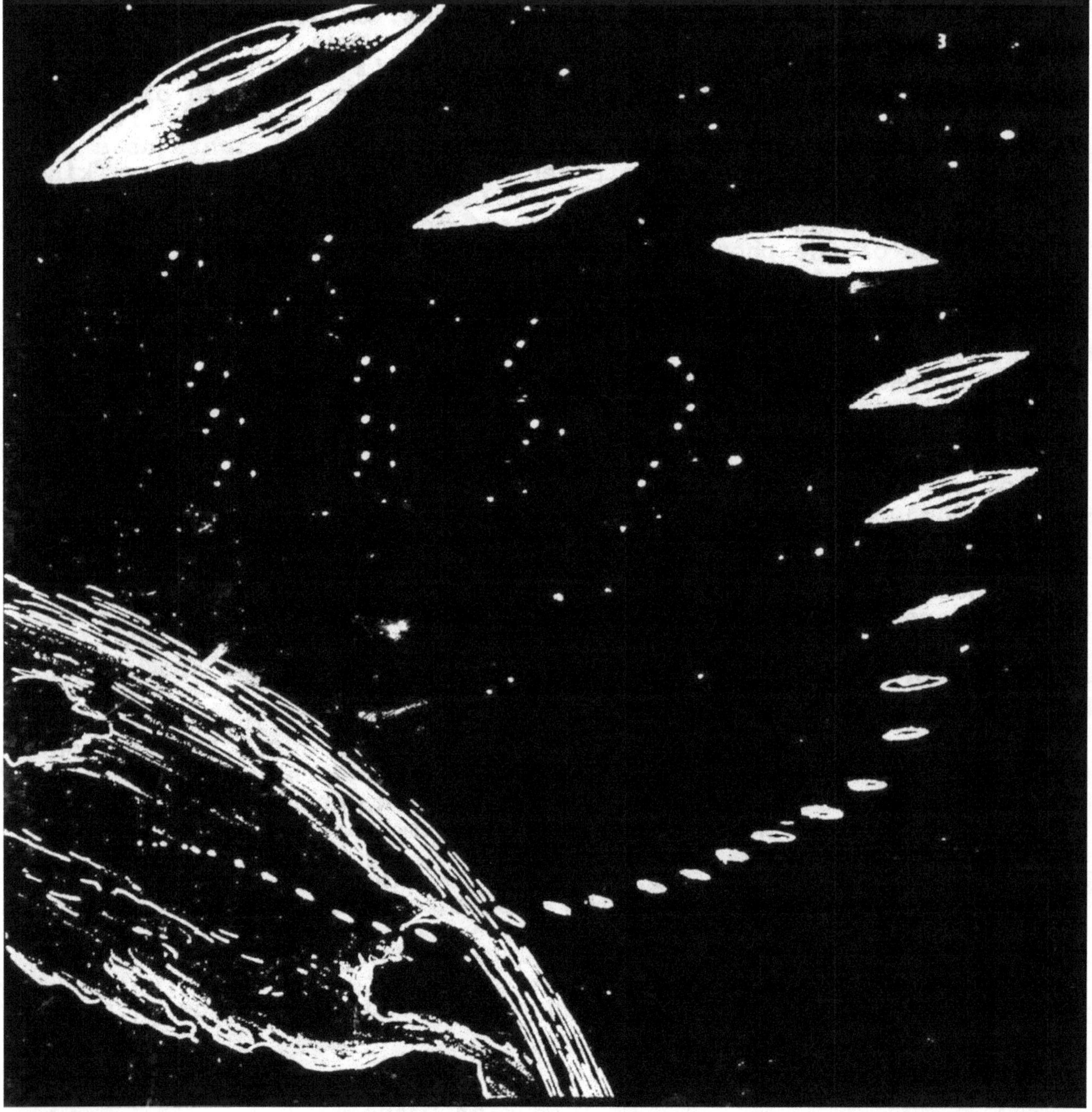

COPY

P.O. BOX 26
PLANETARIUM STATION   N.Y. 24, N.Y.

April 21st 1958

Dwight D. Eisenhower,
The White House,
Washington, D.C.

Dear Mr. President,

      The most important question on many millions of people's minds, not only in this country, but in every nation in the world today, is:- Are we being visited by beings from other worlds? This is not just conjecture, but absolute fact. In a recent poll taken by Hendrix for NICAP, the Washington UFO organization, directed by Major Donald E. Keyhoe, which I'm sure you are well aware of, the percentage determined ONE out of every FOUR Americans believed that FLYING SAUCERS existed. This is no small amount. Hundreds, even thousands of Americans have been trying to get a grown-up answer from the U.S. Air Force, after ten years it's conclusions are as varied as the winds. The only statement that continually crops up is that UFOs do NOT constitute a threat to our security. If this significant statement is true, and the records bear it out to be true, then why the secrecy? Why is the public not being told the facts? Who or what is holding it back? NYSIB, our organization, has covered over fifty of the U.N. Delegates. We have been given the same run-around that our own Authorities have given us. We have proved that it isn't just a conspiracy to withhold the information in this country, but in every country in the world. WHY?

      The President of Brazil recently allowed a picture taken from a Brazilian Naval Vessel in Trinidad, to be released in the Press and a teletype copy of it was released in America, but only by a few local papers. If the Air Force does know the answer and is withholding it, you, Mr. President, as Commander-in-Chief, would endear yourself to the peoples of the world, if you would openly come out with it. This is something far bigger than our own puny planetary squabbles, it's importance second-rates EVERYTHING ELSE. If the A.F. does not know the answer, it's about time the public was given the facts, all of them, and allowed to determine what policy should be followed. Theories that these craft are man-made haven't a leg to stand on, in the light of billions and billions of dollars spent on comparatively obsolete craft as jets, rockets and atomic motors. Whatever the power used by these vehicles is, no country on this planet has it or we'd be efficiently using it.

      Enclosed is a copy of a letter I sent to the N.Y. District Director for Federal Income Tax. It states my case clearly. The letter was read at our last meeting April 19th 1958, with copies ready to be handed to the press. This situation isn't a matter for ridicule any longer, too many top-flight scientists, in every field, air-line pilots, radar men, technicians and people in reputable positions as well as countless thousands, maybe hundreds of thousands, all over the world, of just plain ordinary citizens have seen these craft. You made a statement at one of your press conferences that was televised recently, that there was no palace guard of secrecy in the White House, that you knew everything that was going on, Mr. Eisenhower. Up until now, it has been the conclusion of most everyone in the field, that this withholding of UFO information was entirely on the shoulders of the A.F. If your statement is true, that you do know everything that is going on, then we must assume that you have all the facts to date, and it is by your orders that the information is being withheld. You undoubtedly have your reasons for following this plan of action but secrecy in this situation cannot exist much longer, and in the event of mass landings panic most certainly would be the order of the day, if the people haven't been conditioned beforehand. From the records of a Pentagon Top Secret meeting as far back as January 1953, a scientists' panel urged that the American People be given all UFO information. This recommendation, among others, was officially rejected. Why? We are entering the Space Age now, where man is getting ready to "wet his feet" in outer space. Suppose we are already looked on as the "Juvenile Delinquents" of the Milky Way. As President of an Inter-Galactic Federation, what would you do if you found that Planet Earth was playing around with newly-discovered atomic toys that might possibly upset the balance of your whole system? I leave you to answer this yourself, Mr. Eisenhower. If you are sincere in your desire to bring real peace to this troubled world, not just to America, go before the United Nations and let the world know the true UFO situation, regardless of whether or not you know the answer. This country will make more real friends than all the Lend-Lease help put together has even thought of making. Let us show these visitors from Outer Space that Planet Earth can grow up before it's too late. Other civilizations before us didn't learn their lesson in time, and so we are left with only legends and myths of Atlantis, Lemuria and Mu. NO-ONE can prove they didn't exist, the same applies in reverse. Is this mystery going to be repeated 60,000 years from now? Are people going to argue about whether or not there was once a great continent called America, and discuss the various ways it was devastated? You have the destiny of a planet in your hands, Mr. President, not just a hundred and seventy five million peoples' lives. Don't be swayed by egotists around you, who set up Earth as the Center of the Universe, with themselves as God. On our one dollar bill, series 1957, I see we have finally taken a step in the right direction. It is inscribed "IN GOD WE TRUST". Let whatever or whoever the GOD you trust in be your guiding light, for without spiritual understanding, which has fallen to a dangerous low in this country, we, as a nation are doomed to fall. History is a continuous accumulation of such cases. In the long run, there is only one ultimate weapon; it can overcome all the hydrogen bombs, ICBMs and hate that man, in his childish endeavors can ever hope to conceive; that weapon is LOVE. Love for your fellow man. Without it, we are licked before we start.

A few words from you, could start a new way of life on this planet, regardless of those that thrive on power and greed. They, too, have to return to their maker someday, though they spend their lives trying to prove to themselves they are self-made. Man will have a new goal to look forward to among the stars, but he MUST NOT BE SENT OUT WITH MURDER IN HIS HEART, TO SUBDUE AND CONQUER.

Thank you Mr. President for reading this, and with the hope that we can have a clear-cut answer,

I remain, very respectfully

Douglas Deane, Director.

UFO-mation

Published Quarterly by NYSIB: The New York Saucer Information Bureau

VOL. I WINTER ISSUE NO. I

Published Quarterly by NYSIB: The New York Saucer Information Bureau

VOL. I　　　　　　　WINTER ISSUE　　　　　　　NO. I

NYSIB Re-Dedicates Itself

To those members who did not attend our last meeting on January 31st and who, for various reasons, may have come to believe that NYSIB is now defunct, we wish to say that not only are we still very much alive, but reorganized as well and ready to set about accomplishing our original purpose.

That purpose is, and I quote from the NYSIB Constitution, set forth a year ago (January 1, 1958) by Douglas Deane, our first director: "To (help) stimulate the thinking and reasoning powers of an underestimated citizenry (in every way possible), for the elevation of mankind to its rightful heritage." (and for the understanding of itself and its place in the universe).

Now, in language more specific and down to earth: We,(NYSIB) from this point forward, RE-dedicate ourselves to the joining of forces to all those of similar groups, clubs and interested individuals throughout the world who are seeking to overcome the bonds of fear and superstition.....with desire for truth serving as their spearhead.

As a group so dedicated, we cannot allow ourselves to let this opportunity to slip through our fingers. The time draws nigh and we must reach as many as we can and make them aware that flying saucers DO exist...and put before them the various schools of thought pertaining to this existence! We have the means to do this via our lectures and this publication. Our files are bursting with material and data, and our job lies clearly before us.

To function effectively, in this manner, we as a group must remain objective and unprejudiced. Our job is to serve as an unbiased speaking platform and sounding board for those who have a message; and not to indulge in controversy, theory or speculation.

As individuals, our members naturally have their private convictions. They have, I am certain, come to draw their own conclusions and may be largely in accord with each other regarding the existence of flying saucers and their purpose for being here. Others may not yet be so convinced and may require more conclusive proof and information over which to ponder. This is well, and we are happy to have both sides represented on our membership list...for at least they are thinking.....and listening with open minds and searching hearts.

This, in itself, is an accomplishment, and it now remains for us to unfold, grow, and begin operating on far-reaching scale to help cause this same wonderful thing to happen among as many more people of the world as it is possible for us to do, for TRUTH, if freed from the encumberance of fear, will always speak for ITSELF.

　　　　　　　　　　　　　　　　　　　　Bruce M. Dolen, (Director)

PUBLISHED BY:

The New York Saucer Information Bureau
P.O. Box 26 - Planetarium Station
New York 24, New York

THE STAFF:

Editor..................................John Hay
Art Director & Co-Editor..........Bruce Dolen
Circulation Mgr.
   and Co-Editor................C. Lois Jessup
Production & Gen. Assistant...... Lou Becker

Statements made in this publication are not the official expression of the organization, or its officers, unless stated to be official communications.

SUBSCRIPTION RATES

Single Copies... ¢25 • One Year's Subscription (4 issues, plus supplements.......... $1.00

NOTICE..... NOTICE..... NOTICE

If you, the reader, have any comments to make regarding "UFO-mation," either as to formal or policy, please feel free to make them. In addition, we request that you submit news clippings, articles, sighting reports and any material pertinent to the flying saucer field. All material is subject, of course to editing, since we are cramped for space. We cannot acknowledge receipt of material by mail, and if you should desire that it be presently returned, we ask you to kindly include return postage.

NYSIB OFFICERS

Director................................ Bruce M. Dolen
Secretary..................... Ethel Goldenbergh
Treasurer............................ Lou Becker
Publicity & Lectures..... Constance Lois Jessup
Librarian..................... Adrienne Munkeberg
Sgt. at Arms..................... Hank Dannenberg

NEXT NYSIB MEETING

Saturday, February 28th, 8:00 P.M.
at 50 E. 69th Street - between Madison and Park

Special Attraction

Mr. Gil Wilson, noted muralist, and new member of NYSIB, will give us a preview presentation on a series of color slides telling the story of "Mr. World and the Hue-mans." This is a story of mankind and the atom bomb; and the slides, taken from a series of Mr. Wilson's paintings, depict man's shaky sojourn on this planet down through the ages.

There will be narration by Mr. Wilson and musical accompaniment, and since this presentation has two endings, Mr. Wilson will ask NYSIB members to vote as to which ending they think most appropriate. Afterwards, there will be a short general discussion period with Mr. Wilson presiding, and answering questions.

Mr. Wilson is famous for his paintings illustrating Melville's "Moby Dick," and worked in close collaboration with John Houston, when the movie of that same name was being filmed. Mr. Houston was so intrigued at Mr. Wilson's depiction of the various characters and scenes in the story, that he used them to model his sets and actor characterizations.

REPORT ON ANNIVERSARY MEETING

Our last meeting on January 31st started off with a bang and was conducted in a cool and efficient manner. Since the program included several speakers, all preliminary business was handled and dealt with as rapidly as possible in order to give attending members and friends a chance to relax and listen to the interesting talks of the special guests.

First, Mr. Hans Stefan Santesson, Editor of the well-known science-fiction magazine, "Fantastic Universe," graciously gave a brief but inspiring discourse, sprinkled liberally with his own special brand of candid wit and charm. Mr. Santesson complimented NYSIB on their work, and on the stand they have taken re. Flying Saucers and UFO'S, adding that he himself had that very evening become a member. (A most welcome one too!). He also added that they should not be treated as a joke, but that mankind should face up to the reality of their existence.

Margaret Storm then spoke of her forthcoming publication, "The Return of the Dove;" a story about the late Nicola Tesla.....after which the rest of the evening was turned over to Major Wayne S. Aho, who talked at length and expressed his pleasure at having made this return visit to us after one year, saying; "1959 will be a year of amazing revelations in all fields of UFOLOGY.

He also spoke of his association with O.T. Carr, and demonstrated a model of Carr's OTC-X1 foil space-craft.

to you:

the Man on the Street

Today the average New Yorker must keep his eyes on the STOP and GO signs; walk in squares and, in addition, keep his eyes glued on the flying dollar. Because of fear we are being taxed to death, and there is so little time left for us to LOOK UP.

Subliminal advertising is the subtle sell! With all this going on and TV serving as an opiate for the most rushed man in the world, when *is* he going to find time to LOOK UP?

Our newspapers, loaded with advertising and the familiar daily rapes, stabbings, muggings, hold-ups and crimes of lesser degree--not to mention the cyclic political scandals of both parties--very seldom publish U.F.O. news. Most of it filters in via foreign and domestic U.F.O. pamphlets.*

George Washington is credited with saying that without Thos. Paine's Essays the Revolution could have failed.

Let us hope that the age of reason is not past! Let us have your views as YOU, the Man On The Street see it all. <u>And</u>, support the U.F.O. publication of your choice!

P.S. *NYSIB expects few REPORTS OF SIGHTINGS from its local membership, but those out of town have a better chance to LOOK UP and REPORT. If YOU hear of any reported or unreported sightings, send them to NYSIB, % EDITOR, "UFO-mation." Many many thanks.

and to you:

If one wanders around "live" saucer groups, conventions, lectures, etc., with mouth closed and ears open, one hears a variety of questions loudly argued, or softly whispered by two or more SS people (saucer seekers).

Here are two classic ones:

I. "Do the space men (presumably occupants of intelligently operated U.F.O.'s) contact the Russians?"

This question is motivated by both fear and hope! (a) <u>fear</u> that the Russians might get the edge on us again regarding space knowledge, and (b) <u>hope</u> that a world, changed for the better, lies in the near future.

Spacemen are supposed to love mankind and cherish freedom. Without resolving the question, NYSIB suggests that you read some background material to aid the making up your mind on the obvious direction a "yes" answer to the above question would lead you.

Matter and energy concepts, as related to mathematics, brought on the Atom Age. Time-Space concepts, as related to consciousness, lie still unproved in the eyes of the general public, due to educational failures in the field of Western philosophy; although they are thoroughly expounded in Ouspensky's <u>Tertium Organum</u>, which caused a big intellectual stir in the late thirties. Unfortunately the war obliterated the attention this work deserved, for it has been reviewed as comparable to Sir Francis Bacon's <u>Nova Organum</u>, which changed the world of science then existing in the 17th century.

Ouspensky <u>was</u> a Russian and studied under a Russian by the name of Gurdjieff. He was an occultist, and his book, <u>All and Everything</u>, originally written in Russian and Armenian, is all about the space ship "Karmak."

With tongue in cheek he lampoons every mystical and occult teaching, and aims his barked observations at our human frailties in the world of politics, religion and culture. He offends everyone, unless they have a sense of humor, and the book is in the category of <u>Pilgrim's Progress</u>, and <u>Gulliver's Travels</u>....for the saucer fan who <u>wonders</u> it is a must!

The second question is:

II. "If the space people truly exist and have a message to give to the peoples of the earth, <u>why</u> then, do they pick such illiterate, uneducated people (comparatively speaking, that is) to broadcast and to pass on their message?"

Well, again NYSIB does not attempt to resolve the question; but we <u>do</u> draw your attention to certain facts.

Many people are hearing these contact stories for the first time! Yarns about teleportation, mental telepathy, apports, precipitation and such, that to them may suggest a science far more advanced and wondrous than our Atomic Age. Yet, after the first glow of discovery wears off, and they have perhaps become objects of good-natured scorn from those whom they speak to regarding this new possibility, they turn to the "authorities" for guidance. They <u>must</u>...for they have been regimented to believe only in that authority which holds the lid down on the Pandora's box of uncorrelated scientific tricks..and that <u>lid</u> is stamped TOP SECRET!

Actually, the word "occult" could be applied here; for, if you look in the dictionary, you will see what we mean and pardon the suggestion.

The most convincing aspect of the evidence that some superior intelligence is at work, is the fact that the contactees, as a rule, had no formal knowledge of the occult sciences. Later on, however, most of them had their attention drawn to the reading and contemplation of occult literature and teachings, which only served to strengthen their confidence and prove(to them at least), the logic of that which they had been told...in spite of academic and public ridicule.

(Cont'd page 10)

WHY JOIN NYSIB?
A New Member

This writer finds many good reasons for having joined NYSIB. The paramount "idea fixe" with most U.F.O. groups seems to be to organize, regulate and control the beliefs of the membership and thereby cause them to conform to the assumptions of the organizers as to what the U.F.O.'s really are.

This condition creates two warring camps! The so-called scientific, materialistic, objective school; and the psychic, mediumistic, subjective school. NYSIB, being (as its name implies), a Saucer Information Bureau, sits in both camps with both eyes and ears open for the purpose of gathering information.

NYSIB has recently been accused of proving nothing after one year of life. If it had "proved" anything in so short a time, this writer would be very skeptical. Fortunately, NYSIB seems modest enough not to claim to have solved the riddle of the ages.

Another charge made by some immature brain is that NYSIB is composed of mediums. If this were true it could be considered almost a compliment and should therefore cause new people to come running by the hundreds to join us.....for the reason that in the history of the world, "mediums" have largely changed and directed the course of worldly affairs.

Akhnaton, a mystic visionary, turned Egypt and her hierarchy of lesser gods upside down. Jeanne d'Arc, the maid of Orleans, with the aid of her mystic voices upset Church, State and the Military. This is one of the most intriguing episodes and best documented "odd" event of modern times!

One could, if challenged, continue on ad infinitum...from Nostradomus to Tesla and Jules Verne. To quote James Allen, in his essay, As a Man Thinketh; "The dreamers are the saviours of the world. As the visible world is sustained by the invisible, so men, through all their trials and sins and sordid vocations, are nourished by the beautiful visions of their solitary dreamers. Poet, prophet, sage, and composer of beautiful works of art; these are the architects of heaven. The world is beautiful because they have lived, and without them, laboring humanity would perish."

NYSIB has also been charged as being a do-nothing sewing circle. If by that it is meant that no one person is pushing the others around, with delusions of sterling and self-imagined leadership; authoring by-laws, charter rules and regulations, and in general making a big stir....then that charge is correct! Must one wear a label?

The recent hoax of dissolution could have been successful if there had been a few handy by-laws to manipulate, but by its very nature, that of free association, the day was saved. If you love a mystery, then by all means join NYSIB. You may be the one to discover why someone wants so very badly to see it dissolve like the elusive saucers. So far, for the life of me, I can't.

The U.F.O. in Literature

Apparently those who scream the loudest for Equality and Justice do not intend to share this ideal, for I have attended lectures where any reference to the literature of the past has been shouted down.

Any cross reference to non-present contactees brings on personal condemnation of the absent personage who is not therefore, given the right to defend himself.

NYSIB, in upholding its principles of organization, has sponsored lectures by highly controversial figures, but this does not mean that we (NYSIB), are in perfect agreement with all that is said. This, in itself, would be an impossibility for we as an organization are comprised and made up of individuals; each of which has his or her own ideas (neg. and pos.), regarding the flying saucer field; second, NYSIB is not out to lead them onto a plane of demoralizatia-dogmatica. It is strictly for the individual to decide for himself.

So if we should in the future, (and we will), publish extracts from literature of the past, do not hastily assume that we favor one school of thought over another. No jury should go out for a verdict until all the evidence is in.....and we do mean all the evidence...subjective as well as objective.

The flying saucer search cannot logically begin and end with visual sightings, reports, and verbal testimony on the lecture platform, for this boxes the whole subject into the realm of solely contemporary facts; a sort of isolation booth for the grand prize.

The recognition of this sort of ostrich-like stupidity has brought forth a rash of books covering the historical records from all sources: from the Bible to the books of Charles Forte.

Most of the authors bear the badge of respectability and their findings are considered with respect by the U.F.O. fan who prides himself on not being a member of the so-called "lunatic fringe."

We pride ourselves on being democratic. All parties are supposed to be heard and have their say, and NYSIB supports this worthy ideal. Unfortunately, people assume that because of this unbiased policy, the officers of NYSIB are mediums and soothsayers of one sort or another. This has recently been published as fact!

We ask you to use your natural and God-given intelligence in discerning between the black and the white regarding the field of U.F.O's and to allow your inner voice of reason to speak as clearly as those which seek to confuse and spread the dread fear of free thought.

We ask also that you begin an investigation of your own and perhaps see for yourself whether or not the books and works of such people as Alice Bailey, Madame Blavatsky, Charles Forte and many others (written long before the recently introduced "saucer scare") serve to confirm or condemn that which the contactees of today claim was given to them in good faith by the space people and to be passed along to us.

SAUCER SCIENCE
by John Hay

Many sincere UFO investigators shy away from all subjective aspects of the flying saucer mystery. This, I believe, is due to lack of scientific training in basic research problems.

We hear loud screams from hastily organized investigation groups bearing testimony that they are only concerned with reality! By that, I take it they mean they will go only half way in their research and deal only in actualities.

Any artifax is a materialization of a realization. A realization can be anything from building plans to a complicated electric motor design carried around in the head of an individual. Once transmitted to paper, it (the realization) becomes for the first time an actuality; something that can be understood and shared by other individuals, for from here on the plans easily become artifax. The perfection of the solid, tangible, easily investigated object varies according to the imagination (image-making faculty) of the creative sponsor.

All solid objects, somewhere in time and space, were once merely subjective imaginations: the "reason d'etre" for our inventive section of society; namely the misunderstood inventors. The world's aircraft of today were mostly bauxite less than 50 years ago! Anyone can see, in the short span on one generation, the evolution of a motor car or a TV set. The vast army of "experts" however are, in most cases, only improvers or maintainers, lacking the image-making faculty of the original creator, and have created therefore, the pseudo-science of knowing by hind sight. This is the stumbling bloc in saucer research: knowledge without philosophy, or to put it bluntly, materialism without wisdom.

To properly evaluate reported phenomena about U.F.O.'s, all the sciences must be considered and brought to bear on the subject. This means not only the physical sciences, but also the subjective sciences. Mathematics is a subjective science, and the art of abstract mathematics gave us the equations to create the atom age. These theories have all recently been challenged! This only means that the basic theory must be modified or added to, in the fact of new developments that can't be squeezed into the original narrow concept! This is evolution or growth.

Triangulation can be applied to saucer research, i.e. matter equals energy equals space. If this is true, then so is the reverse or involution: space equals energy equals matter! The condensation, or focus of space, is understood by nearly all school children in the classic example set forth in their textbooks, explaining how the atmospheric condensation into snow, rain or ice, is caused by vibratory changes (temperatures).

What is more materialistic than being hit on the head by a solid chunk of ice from out of the blue? When it melts away and evaporates, only the lump on the head is tangible evidence of what happened. It is so easy to say the man is lying and his wife hit him on the head with a hammer! The yes and no answers to the U.F.O.'s fall into the classic question "Have you stopped beating your wife?" God help you if you never started!

Subjective contacts, (loosely and erronously tabbed "psychic"), unfortunately do not even have the lump on the head as evidence!

Getting back to our equation(M.E.S.): We must classify U.F.O.'s in one box or another, but (and it is a big, overlooked but) we must never forget the common denominator called TIME. Time is related to consciousness and thereby hangs a tale.

The TIME factor deceives the five physical senses. Examples: sound travels with variable speeds according to the medium of transmission. The old rule of thumb is obsolete, i.e.; a cannon fired a mile or two away is heard. An observer calculating between the puff of smoke and his audible reception of the vacuum collapse, uses so many feet per second to gauge the distance. He has used optics, sense of sound, and time. Any one variable in his calculation upsets his final answer. He wants to know the distance between himself and the cannon but if the sound came via radio he is lost. However, if he equalizes the situation by watching the cannon on TV, there is a more complicated situation. Distance has been eliminated, for subjectively he was there! He was made conscious of the whole act, the cannon and its firing. Emplacement of the physical body (his) has no bearing on his awareness.

We in the U.F.O. research are like the man who hears the cannon and trys to calculate the distance and direction of same by sight and sound, and so seek out its location.

Many splendid results and reports have come out of U.F.O. research by civilians. Much phenomena has been explained, but little or nothing has been achieved for the so-called psychic saucer contactee. After studying Project Blue Book, it is obvious that the projected images(drawings)from the descriptive text, are purposely misleading or else executed by people devoid of the image-making faculty. "Sightings (objective and subjective), have dropped off," So says the Air Force. No wonder! Why bother reporting?

Are U.F.O. clubs and researchers the world over going to be guilty of the same error? Are we going to dismiss the subjective contactee as a "lunar-tic?"

If so, close shop! The subjective may become objective. Why? A long time ago R. Shaver made the statement, "They will never catch a saucer unless it (the saucer) wants to be caught."

Is there something to all this? Well, the S.N.A.A.P. orders still hold and recently, during the big newspaper strike in N.Y.C. many New Yorkers read in the Newark Star Ledger that airline pilots were angry at being muzzled. The usual A.F. denials followed, saying that there really is nothing to all this saucer business at all. I agree! There's as little to it as the empty space around us, which is filled with Jack Benny, What's My Line, or Have Gun, Will Travel.

These wierd sounds and pictures, causing these problems to be, are there, all right. Life and time projected for your pleasure, if you have the receiving equipment....... and a subjective, vicarious thrill is provided for again, yes or no! "Vas you there, Charlie?"

Dr. Gonder in the twenties threw a curved ball at astronomy when he propounded his "Curved Light Theory." Space had to be recalculated. Most of us are taught that light travels in straight lines, yet science now uses powerful electro-magnets to direct energy in cyclotrons and light guns. New wonders await us.

Leonardo Da Vinci, one who invented (imaged) prolifically, was a prisoner of the cultural "know-how" of his times. He stated that energy must leave the observer before sight is possible. This is another way of saying that consciousness _radiates_. Man not only receives, but gives energy. When his batteries run down he sleeps; he turns inward and the outer world disappears for him.

How and what does he see in dreams? The subjective world is seen with the mind, and I ask you _not_ to confuse mind with _brain_! This subjective world is the Time riddle we are faced with in the U.F.O. investigation. There is no solid division or yes and no answer, any more than there is a beginning and end to matter, space and energy; just a degree of awareness. We are all familiar with lapsed time films. Imagine if you can, condensation or focus of energy in a fast time cycle, and there you have the disappearing U.F.O's.

In old-fashioned movies the actors only seem to act so quickly. Most of them no longer are here. Did they too disappear in Time?

History repeats the old U.F.O. story, but today we understand it a little better than our ancestors. Hindu legends say that the phenomonal world disappears into paralaya...a sort of world sleep-no dreaming.

The work on the subjective aspect of the U.F.O.s has hardly begun. Not until science probes the man...instead of space...will the answers be turned in! The difference between dreams (thought forms) and true vision must be determined before we dream the subjective contactee with only the lumps on his head that _we_ give him!

Let us part with this thought: the subjective world is real to the artist, the inventor, the dreamer, the abstract mathematician, the true scientist and every common man......if the _latter_ will but admit it. Therefore subjective life (consciousness), needs only a form of energy to help it manifest to our dimension. Be they symbols on paper or bricks and stones, they were once only images in the Mind's eye. What we now know as green may really only be two dots, one yellow and one blue, hetrodyning just for fun!

We can only conclude with the Indian fable about the three blind men who went to "feel" an elephant. Said one, grabbing the trunk, "He is like a snake." Said another feeling the sides, "He is like a wall." Said the other clasping a leg, "He is like a tree." I say, "Look ma, a flying saucer?" She says, "No son, a superman!"

Let flying saucer and UFO fans all be humble enough to admit that while all three blind men were partially right, they were mainly dead wrong! Unless we understand the subjective side of the riddle ourselves, the materialistic answer will never hold fast.

———•———

(EDITOR SPEAKS - Cont'd)

If one is tolerant of past idiots such as Copernicus, Louis Pasteur, Nicola Tesla, Dr. Harvey, Morse, the Wright brothers and a host of others whose names shine brightly in the world of science today; it would be well then to reserve judgement at this time of the saucer lunatic fringe. These people, mentioned above were not considered too bright themselves in the early stages of their respective careers, and were attacked and unmercifully torn to shreds as regarded their morals, characters, financial and social status..and all phases of their private and personal affairs that had no coherent connection with what they were trying to say and do.

The dangerous character is not necessarily the one on the platform, but is quite often the one who circulates among the audience, spreading rumors, ridicule and scorn..and the technique is age-old and shopworn, yet still as effective as it was in the period of time we so ironically call the "dark ages."

The following is an excerpt from a Christmas Message to NYSIB written on Dec. 21, 1958 by Major Wayne S. Aho, Director of Washington Saucer Intelligence.

Major Aho is the "Founding Father" of NYSIB, for it was he who first saw the need for a constructive organization to serve as a public forum in order that lecturers, with ideas and experiences to recount could be heard by the public.

His message reads as follows;

"On the Anniversary of your first year's work, I would like to say to you ....A HIGHER INTELLIGENCE THAN MORTAL MAN'S IS GUIDING AND DIRECTING THROUGH MAN IN THESE PERILOUS TIMES OF PLANET EARTH. ALL WHO WILL HUMBLE THEMSELVES AND ADMIT TO A CREATOR OF ALL... AND TO THE PRESENCE OF ADVANCED BEINGS ON OTHER WORLDS... UPON AND ABOVE THE EARTH, AND ABOUT US, CAN SERVE IN BRINGING ABOUT HIGHER CONSCIOUSNESS.... A HEAVEN ON EARTH. LOVE IS THE POWER THAT REMOES BLOCKS, AND I WOULD ASK YOU TO KEEP THIS IN MIND AS YOU WORK FOR THE GREAT GOAL, FOR YOUR REWARDS WILL NOT BE MORTAL OR OF PRAISE FROM LIPS OF MAN, BUT WILL LEAD YOU TO A GREATER KNOWING OF YOURSELF AND ALL THINGS.... FOR WHAT IS HEAVEN, BUT A HEAVENLY CONSCIOUSNESS, AND A WILL TO SERVE IN EVER GREATER WAYS."

"In the expanding of Earth Consciousness and the growing of man's mind, we all understand that there will be trials and tribulations. It is not an easy task and this is a job for adult minds,... old souls. Let us be ever vigilant."

RECCOMENDED READING

NEW BOOK !   **NEW BOOK !**

"THE COUNCIL OF LIGHTS"

$3.50   by $3.50

George Van Tassel

De Vorss & Co., 516 W. 9th St., Los Angeles, Cal.

New York Saucer Information Bureau
P. O. Box No. 26 Planetarium Sta.
New York 24 N. Y.

VOL. I   SPRING   ISSUE   NO. 2

THE KILLIAN STORY

Capt. Peter Killian was scheduled to appear as the Special Guest Speaker, for N.Y.S.I.B's last Meeting, on March 29th. A last minute phone call from Mrs. Killian to Miss Jessop (N.Y.S.I.B's Lecture Chairman) cancelling the appointment was a disappointment for all Members.

Capt. Killian is employed by AMERICAN AIRLINES, and on the night of February 25, 1959, was pilot of a D-C 6 Passenger Plane, on a scheduled flight, from Newark, New Jersey, to Detroit, Michigan. When flying about 8,000 feet between Philipsberg and Bradford, PA., at 8:45 P.M. he sighted 3 bright whitish lights in a single horizontal line overhead. At first Capt. Killian thought it was the Belt of Orion (a group of stars in a constellation) then taking a second look, he saw both the Belt, and the unidentified objects. These three U.F.O.s escorted the plane for FORTY-FIVE minutes.

After the officials investigated Capt. Killian's report, it was given out by the authorities, that he said "Flying Saucers" were only JETS refuelling in mid-air.

Capt. Peter Killian was then warned not to appear in public and tell his story. Should we comment, "That silence is golden"?

Major Donald Keyhoe, of N.I.C.A.P. Washington, D. C. is making a complete investigation, with the Air Force, on this matter.

PUBLISHED BY:

THE NEW YORK SAUCER INFORMATION BUREAU
P.O. Box 26 - Planetarium Station
New York 24, New York.

THE STAFF:

Editor..John Hay

Co-Editor............................. Constance Lois Jessop

Gen. Assistant..Lou Becker

Statements made in this publication are not the official expression of N.Y.S.I.B., or its Officers, unless stated to be an official communication.

EXCHANGE CO-OPERATIVES:

Dr. Pauline Eastham,
9908 Pershing Drive,
EL PASO, TEXAS.

Saucers Space & Science,
1157 St. Clair Ave., West,
TORONTO 10, ONT. CANADA.

TRUFO, L. E. Lindwig,
4645 W. Adams Street,
CHICAGO 44, ILLINOIS.

U.F.O. Research Bureau
R. R. 3, Danville,
INDIANA, INDIANA.

U.F.O. SCHWEIX,
Nadelberg 31,
BASEL, SWITZERLAND.

SPAN. Jeanne S. Bagby,
521 East 87th. St.,
NEW YORK 28, NEW YORK.

N.Y.S.I.B. OFICERS.

Director................................... Bruce M. Dolen

Asst. Director &
Lecture Chairman .... Constance Lois Jessop.

Secretary............................... Ethel Goldenberg

Treasurer............................... Lou Becker

Librarian............................... Adrienne Munkeberg

Sgt. at Arms...........................Hank Dannenberg

THE EDITOR SPEAKS

The response to the new UFO-mation has been gratifying indeed. There is a great possibility of reforming the ranks of all types of U. F. O. fans against the Secrecy Group that Dr. J. Robert Oppenheimer, Director of the Institute for advanced Study, Princeton University warned against in the New York Times of December 3, 1958. This is mental strangulation of the public mind. This may be necessary in the minds of those "elected" (?) to protect the United States from aggression. This also applies to the other half of our divided world. Ordinary humanity is at the mercy of warring ideologies. Only an informed public can decide the issues thru the ballot. If we are, and it is a big IF, denied the TRUTH about the present world of science and its effects on world economy, then politics will become the master and we the people, the robots of a system that the Constitution of the United States attempts to smash.

The dangerous thinking at high levels is the idea of "Indispensable Man". We as a nation are indeed poverty stricken if there is only one Sherman Adams, and just a single John Foster Dulles. N.Y.S.I.B. does not want to be politic but the danger signals are up! The British press is beginning to rumble about our "sick leaders". Does this condition reflect their thinking? "As a man thinketh so is he" is an ancient truism. The thinking at high levels seems to be that we are not capable or honest enough to manage our own affairs. The tax money must be taken away before it is even handled. The interest is lost by the individual in the State of New York. How soon will this insidious idea spread all over the land?

Why is N.Y.S.I.B. concerned? Because SAGE and other weapons being devised at the Massachusetts Institute of Technology which are "shrouded with super-secrecy" (These are the words of the press, not ours) have developed into a Brain Trust. Fantastic? This is from the Chicago Daily News Service, March 14, 1959. BRAIN MACHINE SEEN DECIDING HUMAN POLICY. Is this some hopped up reporters nightmare?

"An interpretation one scientist here placed on the talk is that a robot brain could make the decision (war) if the President were suddenly incapacitated". There would of course, be no morality or ethics or soul, or what have you, to stop the robot. The only hope in this report was that "Some of the young scientists who are leading the way to the robot era, shudder at the thought of using electronic brain machines for the purpose of destruction..

N.Y.S.I.B. MAIL BAG

So many letters of interest have been received that space does not permit even partial reproduction. The Editor & Co-Editor have replied to them, and also to some old ones ignored by previous officers. Space does not permit many reproductions.

From Switzerland, Lou Zinstag sends U.F.O. SIGHTUNGEN UBER DER SCHWEIZ. We have elsewhere translated a few extracts.

Canada's Gene Duplantier has written and we are reproducing some of his material.

Lawrence E. Lindvig has written that he is ready to co-operate and if members require tapes on U.F.O.S. they should write to L.E. Lindvig 4645 W. Adams St., Chicago 44, Ill.

We received a wonderful letter from Ray Streib of U.F.O. research Bureau R.R. 3 Danville, Indiana. He reports on U.F.O. activity over the Panama Canal Zone. Copies of the U.F.O. NEWS are on file at N.Y.S.I.B. He advises us that the first 'manned rocket ship' has been completed by Convair. The engine is being constructed. As we all know seven planets have been readied by the Government...but no news about the ship.

The New Age Publishing Company has written some very complimentary things about U.F.O.,-MATION.

Mrs. Wm. H. Byrd of 4449, Ranchview Rd. Rolling Hills, California claims to be a "Contactee" anyone interested should write as she is publishing, "WHY WE ARE HERE" at $2.75 by Gloria Lee.

We cannot wind up without mention of Gaylord W. Engle of Rhodes, Iowa a most interesting letter lies dormant in N.Y.S.I.B's files. They have seen U.F.O's and his family are clairaudent. Those interested in the "Contactee" should write to him.

Foreign Sightings

A German UFO paper, "Neuse Europa" writes an article about an EX-Nazi, now in exile in Santiago, Chile. He claims to have been 18 months in a Venusian Space ship, being trained in military supervision by Planetary Hierarchies.

Their aim is to make plans for a New World Republic with Headquarters in Berlin. The Soviet Secret Police makes frequent visits to Santiago Claiming the right to change the Headquarters to Moscow as soon as the Americans evacuate Berlin. An UFO mass landing will follow and all opposition met with a "Death-Ray".

Is this a world conspiracy marching under "Venusian Banner?- The realization of a lunatic "Hitler Dream"?-

For the readers information, the EX-Nazi's name is Karl Michalek, Ahumada 131, Office 110, (Edificie Waldorf), Santiago, Chili.

The "Visitor" published in Detroit, Michigan in the JAN.FEB. March 1959 issue carries many UFO sighting that have occured in Poland.

The Polish "Dookla Swiata" publishes a story about an atomic physicist Olgierd Wolczek and the editor visiting many towns and gathering sightings similar to the U.S. sightings. Apparently the Polish Press is very objective about the reports and does not indulge in ridicule. N.Y.SI.B is very fortunate to have these translated articles along with the sketches made apparently by Editor Neugebauer. He also made taped recordings and signed interviews. A tip of the hat to Editor Neugebauer of the Polish Weekly "Round The World"

This answers our question in the last issue.."Do flying saucers appear behind the iron curtain. In Polish the saucers are called "Latajace Talerze" As U.F.O. Study Clubs exist in Poland we intend sending a copy of UFOmation to Editor Neugebauer.

In June 1958 a mysterious blast occured in one of the main traffic sections near Carrara in Northern Italy.

The stormwindows in some of the trains broke into pieces and fell into a nearby swamp. Even the heavy glass windows in Omnibusses suffered considerable damage causing injury to many passengers. The accidents remain unsolved.

FOREIGN NEWS.

Your Editor received copies of SAUCER, SPACE & SCIENCE edited by Gene Duplantier, 1157 St. Clair Ave. West, Toronto 10, Ontario, Canada. We reprint some extracts because they confirm some of our conclusions re space ships versus saucers.

-E X T R A C T S-

BRITAIN FAR ALONG ON DEVELOPMENT OF FLYING SAUCER

London, Jan. 26 (Reuters)--Britain has taken the wraps off a secret project which may win an international race to develop the world's first flying saucer vehicle.
This would be a major step to smooth "magic carpet" travel over land & sea. The National Research Development Corp. here has announced that Britain's flying saucer, or hovercraft, designed to ride a cushion of air above water, has reached such an advanced stage of construction that a piloted version might be tested "within a few months."
Credit: Dough Mapes; Buffalo Evening News, Monday, Jan. 26, 1959.
Meanwhile, back at Malton, Ontario, home of Canada's flying saucer, the AVRO Aircraft Company had to lay off 13,800 workers because of the cancellation of the CF-105, better known as the AVRO Arrow. However, it is known that work and development will continue on the vertical take-off flying saucer project for the U.S. Air Force. (SeeP. 6)

The Russian's biggest newest secret weapon is an atomic ray gun. The gun's rays can cut boulders like butter...The top defense brass, including Secretary of Defense, Neil McElroy, will fly to a new secret missile launching base in the Pacific in April. The U.S. plans to try another shot at the moon from this new base.

BLAMES FALLOUT FOR STRIPED COWS

London, (Reuters) Jan. 26, 1959--Radioactive fallout now has got the blame for raising zebra stripes on cows. Welsh farmer Maurice Thomas plans to sue the government for compensation for the damage done to his pedigreed herd by nuclear tests, according to the Sunday newspaper "The People". The cows' hair fell off in strips.

The U F O IN LITERATURE

Classic literature is timeless like all the arts. It contains TRUTH beyond the limitation of current fashion. Time and time alone decides what is durable, and therefore timeless. A man like Marcus Aurelius holds more respect from modern man than many a modern dictator, when he writes

> "Love the art, poor as it may be, which you have learned, and be content with it; and pass through the rest of your life like one who has with his whole soul entrusted to the gods all that he has, be neither tyrant or slave of any man."
>
> Marcus Aurelius 161-180 A. D.

This is a voice from the past espousing freedom for the individual. He was not a christian so his reference no modern psychologist would reject. Aurelius by many scholars, is considered fatalistic, melancholy, whistling in the dark. "Despite the unreasonableness of men and events, there is a deeper REASON which is good, a reason which is God". (This last quote is from a modern writer, not believing in gods, but a God). Such thoughts about Aurelius become suspect if the "Elohem" is considered in reference to creation of a planet. Space contactees claim there is a hierarchical system in the Universe. Perhaps Marcus Aurelius was not far off the beam when he stated: "If a fault is in your own power to correct, why do you persist in it? But if the power is in another, whom do you blame—the ATOMS or the GODS? Both are foolish. You must blame nobody. If you can, correct the cause.." Things have changed since his day. We do have a say in the affairs of men. How foolish is an electronic BRAIN. Who or what is our God? These are burning questions of the Day. (See editorial)

Down thru the ages man has sought an escape hatch either by solar boat, flying horse, solar chariot, thunderbird or solar ship. Suggested reading on this last item and U.F.O. in general, is the OAHSPE, a New Bible by Dr. John Ballou Newbrough 1882 A.D. Saucer fans will be surprised to find how old is this problem of ATOMS and GODS.

SAUCER SCIENCE

By John Hay

CANADIANS REPORT ON RUSSIAN MEDICAL PROGRESS

Too little information about Russia reaches the general public. It is deplorable that the reports of our own Flying Saucer stories are apparently suppressed by the press but what about Russian contacts? Are certain Russians getting and acting upon 'Space Help' ? The theme has been that the Space People see no division in humanity as we do. They want to help all dwellers on the dark planet Shan (Earth) but only with positive and constructive ideas and principles. George Van Tassel claims to have received health principles to date no one seems to pay serious attention. Is there opposition? Out of Russia comes a new approach to health.

There is a strange similarity to the stories and the yoga methods, especially hatha and rajah yoga. Perhaps we should re-read George Adamski?

Two Canadians Charlotte and Dyson Carter spent considerable time in Russia in clinics and at the U.S.S.R. Psychiatry Institute with a Dr. P. E. Beilin. They report:

Dr. Beilin after considerable orthodox opposition (same as here) 'discovered', as a medical researcher from the Ukraine (that is we suppose equivalent to 'from the sticks') and demonstrated that the body and mind can be healed by 'sleep! Sleep without drugs. Sleep against pain. Sleep without hypnosis.

Artificial moonlight to heal with sleep. Sleep with color and pictures. This is not the ordinary sleep of fatigue. Of course this is very inexpensive.

One giant step claimed by the Russians is proof that babies and alcohol just do not mix before birth. Perhaps that is why Khruschev clamped down on vodka...except for grandpas! Baby raising always seem to forecast war, if it becomes the concern of a Napoleon or a Hitler.

Another 'discovery' is that the skin is the most important muscle in the body. It can be exercised sitting down and controlled to give perfect health. (All yogis take a bow) Then there is the topic of 100 year olds...only 200 years to go to catch up to the beautiful Space Girls!

It is also claimed the Russian advances against Cancer are greater than their Sputnik and Satellite successes. IF this is so, will we hear about it belatedly, like the Sputnik news? We saw it in the skies above and the next day we saw news pix of Russian dogs in training. Pictures that MUST have been censored, lying in files, hoping against hope that the Russians would fail before we succeeded.

The Public is learning the hard way...by shock. All is not gold that glitters. We should like to know if there are any space or U.F.O. clubs in Russia or are the Tibetans teaching them a thing or two about vimanas and dorjes?

While we take tons of sleeping pills the Canadians claim they are the first visitors to have studied and tried the amazing new natural health methods with success. Incidentally it is Dyson Carter MSc., F.R.C.G.S., M.C.L.C. and his wife Charlotte Carter R.N., P.H.N. They are qualified and recognized medical writers above suspicion from the silence boys.

NEWS FLASH

Since writing the article about the Canadian Investigation of Soviet Health Studies and the conjecture that Yoga was involved, we expected the ridicule group would loudly' haw haw' such ideas. The following from the Journal American of March 17th. 1959 is worth quoting:-

REDS EYE YOGI FOR 'SPACEMAN'

New Delhi, India (UPI) Soviet scientists are turning to one of the East's oldest practices, Yoga, in their efforts to conquer space. (Since the above was written news has been 'released' about the Tibetan revolt).

SPECIAL TRANSLATIONS

By Adrienne Munkeberg

January 7, 1959, <u>Evening Post</u>, Norway

A young man from Granddal near Sandnes had a strange experience on Saturday afternoon about 14.30 o'clock (2:30 p.m.) which he tells the Rogaland newspaper. While working outside to get his wood into the house he heard a peculiar sound as of a flock of birds. A bullet-like flat object, probably a flying saucer landed on a hill a short distance away. A tall well-built dark brown man stepped out. A strange color combination on his hands and face was noticeable, the brown being predominant as a background. Another distinct characteristic was his helmet to which an antenna was attached. He walked along a narrow path; advancing closer, about 100 meters away, the observing young man who had hid himself and was lying still would have run away if the mysterious stranger had come closer. But he turned around and went back to his flying saucer. The whole experience lasted about 15 minutes.

This is an overall picture of the young man's story. He is know to be a very calm and sober-minded man, and absolutely reliable. The police force has been notified, newspapermen have searched the "Sola" (airport) but no helicopter was over the Granddal area at that time.

The policeman at the station in Sandnes said in his interview with "aftenposten" that we cannot just overlook the whole case as a figment of imagination, but search for a clue. Together with military experts we will search the spot for an eventual clue or mark. He said: "The young man who has seen the phenomena is absolutely strong and healthy with a sober and sound mind. For many years he has worked in a bicycle factory in Sandnes. He first told his collegues what he had seen. He did not notify the police, nor the newspaper for fear of being disbelieved. I believe the description he gave us of the flying saucer fully agrees with other information about flying objects seen a nd observed over the country. They are flat, about 7-8 meters in diameter." says the policeman.

<u>U.F.O.-MATION SUBSCRIPTION, ONLY</u>, $1.00 per annum, (
   Four issues.

TRANSLATIONS FROM NORWEGIAN NEWSPAPERS Cont:
By Adrienne Munkeberg

The German Society for Rocket Technique and Space Research held their annual meeting in Frankfurt. The well-known scientist, Dr. Heinrich Faust said in his lecture "Teachings of the Atmosphere for Future Space Travel" that we are convinced of the existence of other artifical moons and vanguards throughout space, built and operated by intelligent beings from other planets, although we have not yet been able to prove their existence. The physicist, Mr. W. Pons, agreed on this, and said we must be able to accept the probability that life on earth is not a coincidence in cosmic development. The fact that we are not yet able to visit or communicate with inhabitants of other planets does not mean that they cannot visit us. It would be wrong and foolish to assume that space people need be on a lower level of development than we are. The "showing off" even in assuming we have cosmic supremacy is always a sign of an inferiority complex.

OBITUARY

N.Y.S.I.B., Regrets to announce the " PASSING " last month, of PROF. MAURICE K. JESSUP, famous Astronomer and Scientist. DR. JESSUP was very interested in " FLYING SAUCERS " and wrote several books on the subject. the most outstanding were, "U.F.O.ANNUAL" and "THE EXPANDING CASE FOR THE U.F.O." We extend our sympathy to his Family at this time, for their loss.

N.Y.S.I.B., MEMBERSHIP, $4.00 per annum, payable

at the rate of $2.00 every six months, JANUARY,/ JUNE.
(includes U.F.O. MATION.)

RECOMMENDED READING

NEW BOOKS.   NEW BOOKS.

FROM OUTER SPACE TO YOU, by HOWARD MENGER............ $4.50.
    Saucerian Publications, Box 2228, Clarkesburg, W. VA.

RETURN OF THE DOVE, by MARGARET STORM............... $5.00.
    Margaret Storm Publications, 2502 N. Calvert ST,
                    Baltimore, 18, MD.

A CALL AT DAWN, by KELVIN ROWE,...................... $3-50.
    Understanding Publications Co, 101 S. Lexington St.,
                    El Monte, California.

Return Postage Guaranteed

New York Saucer Information Bureau

P.O. Box 26
Planetarium Station   N.Y. 24, N.Y.

PRINTED MATTER

UFO-mation

Published Quarterly by NYSIB: The New York Saucer Information Bureau

VOL 1   SUMMER ISSUE   NO 3

Published Quarterly by NYSIB: The New York Saucer Information Bureau

| VOL I | SUMMER ISSUE | NO 3 |

N.Y.S.I.B. LECTURES.

Despite the hot and humid weather in N.Y.C., on THURSDAY and FRIDAY AUG. 27, 28, 1959, 121 persons attended N.Y.S.I.B.LECTURES, at 211 WEST 57 ST., and Hotel Ansonia, Broadway & 73 ST. to hear SANTIAGO VELASQUEZ' interesting account of his experiences, which led to the publishing of " WORDS OF WISDOM."

ALL DAY FLYING SAUCER RALLY JAMBOREE.

SUNDAY, SEPTEMBER 27, 1959, UNIT #14, of "UNDERSTANDING" (DAN F

SUNDAY, SEPTEMBER 27,1959, UNIT #14, of "UNDERSTANDING" (Dan Fry's Group)sponsored the above RALLY, at the Studio of MARIANNA BEST, 838 PARK PLACE, BROOKLYN, N.Y. About sixty persons were present believers and skeptics sat around and listened to the Scheduled Speakers. ANDY SINATRA's "Astral Projection Stories" was ridiculed by the skeptics, but delighted the Neophytes, and accepted by the true Mystics.

    REV. FRANK STRANGER, spoke briefly about U.F.O.SIGHTINGS old and new, which he has recorded in his book "SAUCERAMA".

    DR. HENRY TUDOR MASON,(President of World Faiths,Inc)gave an inspiring talk on how to achieve UNDERSTANDING. and his well chosen words, spoken as "one having authority" seemed to chase out all negative influences, by his positive vibrations

    HANS STEFAN SANTESSEN,(Fantastic Universe) after a short talk giving the interesting angle, of an Editor's dilemma in trying to present Flying Saucer material, acted as Moderator of the Forum, and handled the question and answer period,with his usual tact, wit, and courtesy.

    ELLERY LANIER's (Long John's Party Line Panalist) interpretation of Prof. Carl Jung's Book "Flying Saucers a Modern Myth" presented a balanced concept,which was refreshing.

    MRS. BEST, (an excellent Hostess) presided graciously,and after the Speeches, offered a beautifully prepared Dinner (Buffet Style)to those who remained for further friendly discussions. Many N.Y.S.I.B. and N.I.C.A.P. Members were there to enjoy this happy andinstructive day.   C.L.J.

PUBLISHED BY:

THE NEW YORK SAUCER INFORMATION BUREAU
P.O. Box 26 - Planetarium Station
New York 24, New York.

THE STAFF:

Editor..John Hay

Co-Editor................................ Constance Lois Jessop

Gen. Assistant.....................................Lou Becker

Statements made in this publication are not the official expression of N.Y.S.I.B., or its Officers, unless stated to be an official communication.

EXCHANGE CO-OPERATIVES:

Dr. Pauline Eastham,
9908 Pershing Drive,
EL PASO, TEXAS.

U.F.O. Research Bureau
R. R. 3, Danville,
INDIANA, INDIANA.

Saucers Space & Science,
1157 St. Clair Ave., West,
TORONTO 10, ONT. CANADA.

U.F.O. SCHWEIX,
Nadelberg 31,
BASEL, SWITZERLAND.

TRUFO, L. E. Lindwig,
4645 W. Adams Street,
CHICAGO 44, ILLINOIS.

SPAN. Jeanne S. Bagby,
521 East 87th. St.,
NEW YORK 28, NEW YORK.

N.Y.S.I.B. OFICERS.

Director................................. Bruce M. Dolen

Asst. Director &
Lecture Chairman .... Constance Lois Jessop.

Secretary................................ Ethel Goldenberg

Treasurer................................ Lou Becker

Librarian................................ Adrienne Munkeberg

Sgt. at Arms............................Hank Dannenberg

THE EDITOR SPEAKS

Governor Rockefeller is going to push legislation to enforce by law the building of "fallout shelters" in every home in New York State. This will be a neat tie-in with the Supreme Court decision that a "Health Inspector" may enter any home in the United States without a warrant.

The Spirit and Soul of 1776 is being driven out of the body of 1959.

The literature predicting a police state, here in the U.S.A., that passes over our desk to N.Y.S.I.B.'s files is rather ridiculous until one reads of such proposed legislation. Even without going into the legal implications of such residential and private property control, it is very obvious somebody is confused about atomic debris.

1. Space contactees such as George Van Tassel, Adamski, George King, et al have all predicted and warned about atomic poisoning.

As a matter of fact we would not be "bothered" by such ancient things as u.f.o.'s if we were still in the gunpowder stage!

2. The Press--New York Times, March 19, 1959:

"Senator Clinton P. Anderson, Dem. N.M. accused the Def. Dept., of 'gagging' the committee on information because it was contrary to what the A.E.C. had previously said, and would upset some of those running around saying fallout is no more dangerous than the luminescent dial on a watch."

Gov. Rockefeller of course can not be too concerned about this type of fallout. He must be thinking of wartime fallout!

Happy optimist that he and others would be world leaders are, they think that someone will win the next world war.

3. To add to the confusion this headline refutes the Senator and the political ambitions and opportunity of a Rockefeller to both save our money and our bodies.

"EXPERT BLASTS HYSTERIA ON FALLOUT PERILS" Washington, July 20, 1959 in the N.Y. Daily News.

J. H. Morse Jr., Assistant to the Chairman of the A.E.C., J.A. McCone, states that high officials (Governors?) are scaring us to death with security. As a result of secrecy on fallout information (the pot calling the kettle black?) he intimates it is not as bad as it is "imagined." He winds up his speculations with the bright idea to make smaller bombs to confine wars to limited areas!!!

(Continued on Page 49.)

N.Y.S.I.B. MAIL BAG

Geo. Van Tassel advises he will not put Proceedings in book form as he did the 1936-39 issues. This is important we think as many will find the first 3 vols invaluable as a reference book of these years. If you want to help him change his mind write to Geo. Van Tassel, P. O. Box 458, Yucca Valley, Calif.

V.C.S.E.G.W.M. (Herb Clark) P.O. Box 650, Sta. A. Vancouver, B.C., Canada offers tape transcripts of an address by Dr. Wm. Davidson, Co-chairman of the Atomic Scientists of Chicago. Subject: The Challenge of the Nuclear Age. $3.00 It will give you nightmares. Ed.

In the last issue we saw L. E. Lundvig was "ready to co-operate". A recent letter questions this meaning. Please understand Mr. Lundwig is an independent to us and all that was meant was that he has tapes available for our readers!

July 28, 1959 Herb Clark writes, "We are forwarding some of the issues of our bulletin sheet and hope you may find something of interest in them. We appreciate your 'liberal' attitude towards the landing and contact reports. In fellowship, Herbert D. Clark, Secretary, U.A.F.S. Club". These are excellent bulletins.

Howard Kaufman, 5302-1/2 Vantage Ave., North Hollywood, Calif. writes that he wants pictures of ghost rockets, world War II or 1959. Maybe he means foo-fighters? Anyone care to help him out?

We received a request for info about the Soviet Health Studies. This is being answered.

July 28, '59 by air (where has this been?) C.I.C.O.A.N.I. Hulvis B. Alexis C Postal 1. 675 Belo Herrizonte (a hotel) Brazil writes "We shall be delighted to exchange information with you" It was addressed to a Douglas Deane.

Aug. 6, 1959. The Little Listening Post writes "We would appreciate any news about N.Y.S.I.B. -- how many members, how are the meetings, any lectures concerning sightings, etc."

(Attention officers of N.Y.S.I.B. Ye editor does not have such facts.)

NEW EXCHANGE CO-OPERATIVES.

HERBERT CLARK,
V.A.F.S.C.,
BOX 720, STATION A,
VANCOUVER. B.C., CANADA.

THE HON. BRINSLEY le POER TRENCH,
FLYING SAUCER REVIEW,
1 DOUGHTY STREET,
LONDON, W.C.1., ENGLAND

SIGHTINGS.

News blackouts exist apparently regarding the subject of U.F.O.'s. Did anyone in the New York area see in print the following?

July 11 (UPI) Honolulu "Crews of five airliners startled". The Los Angeles Evening Herald Express carried on it's mast in two inch type..."PHANTOM SPACE LIGHTS SEEN BY PACIFIC PLANES". On July 16th the Oakland Tribune, Oakland, Calif. carried on it's masthead two inch type proclaiming..MYSTERY SKY LIGHTS SIGHTED.

Six sheriff's deputies, Stockton airport officials and numereus residents watched crescent shaped objects, carrying lights that blinked, hover from 1:25 a.m. to 2:30 a.m. when they disappeared. They ranged from white to orange in color. When a plane appeared they seemed to signal each other by blinking their lights. Deputy Van Sant and Max Benitez kept watch until they were joined by Deputy Robt. Jones and Clyde Skogland. We wonder if the A.F. will charge the sheriffs with being drunk?

Captain George Wilson, 43 of Seattle, Wash. a 19-year veteran who flew the DC/7C from San Francisco, was visibly shaken by his experience as was his co-pilot and flight engineer, Robt. Scott, who left his mouth open on the Honolulu trip! We will soon run out of reliable pilots who don't drink or have hallucinations. Anyway, it was probably crazy irresponsible R.C.A.F. pilots flying their atomic crescent shaped plane that mysteriously disappeared or blew up.

All this is a feather in Gabe Green's hat as he said "they" would show--and they did--and how.

Canadian Pacific Airlines saw them also as did Slick Cargo Airways.

Gabe Green's "AFSCA" (Amalgamated Flying Saucer Clubs of America,Inc.) and Geo. Van Tassel's "Proceedings" both print a most unusual picture. A Sheriff, symbol of our lack of self-control, took a picture, with his polaroid camera, of Giant Rock. He was surprised at what he saw in the print. So he took another pix, but it was not unusual. The picture we refer to is a picture of Reserve Sheriff of San Bernardine County, Calif., in full planetary regalia and badge holding his two polaroid pixs. One shows the allqged space ship and or force field. The other taken about 5 mins. later shows only a plain view.

It is unusual as most "policy" officers will not get involved in such doings! We wonder if he is retired--now? (Since writing this we heard about the 6 Stockton Sheriffs.)

FOREIGN NEWS.

From the Vancouver Clubs fine bulletins (Nov. '58 issue) we quote, "In April of 1958 the Roman Catholic Church appointed a commission of leading theologians to study the duties of the church towards creatures in outer space. This came at the heels of a closed meeting of the Pontifical Academy of Sciences in the Vatican." Page Geo. Van Tassel, Adamski and Williamson! Our Lady of Fatima has been raising heaven? Is she a space lady? Ric Williamson intimated the Italians and Romans were jolted by space phenomena all thru 1958.

The author of the book La Pluralite des Mondes (1688) is more up to date and open minded than most of the so-called scientific ufo clubs that readily believe in the "night side" contactees who because they are frightened, negative and reluctant to tell of their contacts with green gnomes or hard shelled dwarfs with silica skins are supposed to be more reliable than the optimist "day side" contactees. To us it is all the Madison Ave. touch! The hard and the soft sell. If you think hard enough and have a classical education you will realize just what this hokey pokey is all about!

WE SEE BY THE PRESS

ST LOUIS MARCH 18-50 (U.P.I.)

School childred in metropolitan St. Louis are participating in a drive to collect 50,000 baby teeth a year to measure the amount of strontium 90 absorbed by growing children.

COMMENT

We were all assured years ago that there was no danger from fallout...but now with increased dirty fallout plus secret outer space explosions we get it in snow, drinking water, plant food, animal food. Each step is accumulative.

With the news release of outer space explosions the U.S. claimed "top Secret", but many people reported strange explosions (air force denials) echoes and flashes in the sky. Officially no reports of phenomena were turned in. Rumours flew around however of outer space battles!

In view of all this and the "stories" the contactees tell about spacemen cleaning up our "deadly Debris" one would think they would go away in disgust.

The U F O IN LITERATURE

The U.F.O. search is bogged down! The sightings remain the same, aloof and elusive. However law enforcement officers seem to be more involved lately as witnesses. Is this a plan? The government keeps the lid on its box of magic and the Pentagon claims all is "hallucination". This is why sheriffs are being rounded up by space craft?

The original pattern as discovered by Keyhoe and other respectable civilian investigators has not changed and most U.F.O. clubs are duplicating. Nothing new has come out of their research, only two cold conclusions

1. There is 'something' in the sky besides the junk and debris we throw up for celestial garbage.

2. The majority of U.F.O. fans (90%) are nuts and have fallen into the religious revelation class.

N.Y.S.I.B. files show that most U.F.O. clubs depend on each other for news. Anything new comes out of contactee stories. It would be quite dull without them!

Recently the N.Y. Daily News featured four articles that fairly well summed up the average persons ideas about space ships and their reality.

Most occult literature refers to space ships or something akin to the "flying angels" or foo-fighters. Long before the ufo's made news one occult writer told of a space ship buried beneath the Great Pyramid of Giza. (What a chance for Nasser!)

We often wonder how many of the contactees have read some or all of this material. We find space ships in Theosophy, Hinduism and all primitive religions and cultures, so it is not hard to find belief in space travel, communion between planets, etc. Along with this we find a belief in man as

1. A material substance (molecular)
2. A ghost or astral substance (electric)
3. A spirit or mind alone (mind or atomic)

However these patterns repeat at all levels as does the search for the building block of matter. On earth man could exist as all three in one or one at a time, but on a hot star only as number 2 and 3. In uncondensed space he could exist as only number 3 or as a god-like being. The ability to leave his physical body is the basis for all this belief.

Is the U.S. Government interested in such nonsense? Yes! We advise you to read Dr. Andy Puharuch's book, "The Sacred Mushroom" and learn for yourself. If every ufo fan does, then the search will be on again and the contactees will come into their own, instead of being supercilliously classified as sick men and women!

Continued on Page 47.

SAUCER SCIENCE

By John Hay

If one wishes to take an objective view of the subject of flying saucers, U.F.O.'s, space craft or celestial visitors (take your choice of designation) one cannot ignore the impact and reaction on the public mind. In other words, the visual and mechanically recorded sightings along with testimony which may be true or false, have been fairly well evaluated by research groups the world over and it is not enough. It leads nowhere. The official position of the Government Agencies is still the same. There are objects, material or immaterial in the skies that are unidentified. Most U.F.O. clubs who keep clear of the subjective material have come up with no better answers than those given by the government! And why should they? It all reminds one of a fly on a windowpane who keeps buzzing around one spot and hasn't sense enough to crawl up and over the open top!

The official stand by policy making groups is, that due to the fact that our present day science cannot find intelligence outside of our planet it therefore does not exist officially! This was well pointed up on the Alcoa C.B.S. U.F.O. show of January 22, 1958 when Dr. Menzel stated we would eventually go out into space but nobody would ever come in!

It is debatable whether this is a logical conclusion or just a religious hangover as both Christian and Jews, (the bulk of our western culture) are bedeviled by this same question as a religious issue.

Elsewhere you will read of the Roman Catholic action as a result of outer space activity. Needless to say the subjective side of man has always been recognized by the Mother Church but its relation to the space age is an unformulated dogma as yet apparently, except so far as Mary was translated bodily to heaven. Geo. Van Tassel would say by a transistor beam to a space ship and away!

It would seem then that the battle for recognition in the public mind is between pure materialism, no hanky panky, and the subjective method.

Materialism being a science and subjectivism being an art, it is obvious where the battle would end in the public mind. Except for one strange undeniable fact. The U.F.O.'s have not alligned themselves _publicly_ with either faction! They still keep coming and a goin'. Like Jacob's dream, the angels ascend and descend. This we hasten to say does not mean that there are not some people who "_claim_" to have authority from space brothers.

SAUCER SCIENCE

By materialistic standards most of the contactee's have not proved their claims--but and this *is* the point of this article, the outcome of all this is an intensified activity and interest by everyone in subjective matters. The revelation to be is that there is a science to subjectivism. We can see this in attempts to rationalize E.S.P. and a renewed interest in research by such projects as carried on by Dr. Puharich. When such projects become respectable, people will take an intelligent interest in occultism which will no longer be occult but a revelation!

As we are in a predicting mood let us state that one day people will watch a man disappear on their TV sets and it will not be a trick with cameras! Few people will believe it but many will accept the explanation. Light can be magnetised, is magnetic and can be bent. This explains Dr. Gonder's Curved Light Theory and is the reason why astronomy goofs so much!

Since writing the above, we learn Long John Neble of W.O.R. Party Line fame has seen this phenomena. Some trick, eh John!

Let us recall the fact that Geo. Van Tassel claimed at a N.Y.S.I.B. lecture that *he* held a spaceman's hand and the space man disappeared, yet he could feel him!

Andy Sinatra also claims a man was transparent in his barber chair!

Draw up a chair, Long John!!

N.B. See October **Fate** **Magazine** for Long John's confession!

U. F. O. IN LITERATURE (Cont.)

We are not being facetious when we say Mr. Sick is a "well man"!

The Japanese authorities say Mr. Hwang Hyun Sick is sane in spite of the fact that he claims he boarded an egg shaped, silver coloured craft by invitation (like George Van Tassel) from three men and three women dressed in blue business suits, like Americans They were blond (sandy) and blue-eyed but had Chinese features! The men were tall, about 6 ft. Mr. Sick talked to a gal in Japanese. We can hear loud guffaws about Mr. Sick's sick libido and his wishful thinking. We could agree except for a strange co-incidence--Marco Polo writes of such creatures met during his journeys to far Cathay and Tartary!

Mr. Sick's story is in the Vancouver F.S. Club's bulletin we quote it to show how Marco Polo's story makes Mr. Sick's story more acceptable. Harb Clark please note.

SPECIAL TRANSLATIONS
By Adrienne Munkeberg

From the Danish UFO News, August 1959:

Dr. Alberto Perego of Rome, Italy makes the following statement as reported in the Danish UFO News:

"Thousands of UFOs from Mars and Venus are continually circling the Earth to prevent an atomic war. All the governments of the world knew that at least 50,000 UFOs have been observed and that over 4000 landings have taken place.

"The reason for its secrecy is a non-interference in the political affairs of the world for fear of panic.

"The UFOs' mission is to prevent any single nation from becoming too powerful."

Dr. Perego also states that there is ample proof that six American planes were forced to land on a space platform and the 22 pilots were later on sent back to earth to relate to authorities all that had taken place.

SIGHTINGS (Cont.)

The pix the officer took has been enlarged and is printed in both journals. This occurred on May 24, 1959.

The best picture of Sheriff, Ackerman of 29 Palms, Calif. is the picture in the AFSCA souvenir brochure. However, George Van Tassel's Proceedings explain in detail the circumstances and seem to also hit the nail on the head with respect to our economy. Leading editorials have recently supported his views.

A prophecy made on the Jack Parr show Aug. 25 '59 is that the U.S. will devaluate the dollar. Nuff said George!?

The Vancouver Council of Social Engineering (P.O.Box 650, Sta. A, Vancouver B.C., Canada) reports that Reinheld Schmidt's story of seeing Russian underwater installations for missile warfare (while on his recent trip to the pole in a Saturnian space craft) has been verified recently by Robert S. Allen's report that the U.S. and Canadian Navies have discovered radioactive datum plates for markers at 1,000 ft. under, so that subs can accurately fire I.C.B.M.'s.

So that is why Russian Trawlers snagged the trans-Atlantic cables?

Another contactee seems to have rung an "alarum" bell!

THE EDITOR SPEAKS, (Cont.)

Just a little bit dead, eh? (See or hear Dr. Wm. Davidson's lecture as advertised elsewhere here.) None of the above makes sense, yet we are captive to it all because of security or politics or just plain evil.

No wonder nations have a suicidal tendency. No wonder individuals lose all sense of direction and become ripe for the robot age! The only important people left are the politicians and force boys. No wonder such stories as we printed in the last issue of UFO-mation about a "New Berlin" under invading Venusian Banners get a response, for it was just such an atmosphere that bred Hitlerism to fill a vacuum.

We hear serious U.F.O. researchers saying the contactees are not to be believed. All we can say is that at least they are consistent on one point -- fallout!

4. Compare the point 3 (July 20th A.E.C. release) with the August 27th '59 Herald Tribune (AP) headline

"MORE DATA ON FALLOUT DEMANDED. IT'S MORE RAPID THAN EXPECTED" More rapid than the "experts" expected but way back when the U.F.O.'s were supposed to be releasing green balls to clean the atmosphere. Without reprinting the article let us quote parts. "The threat from atomic radiation fallout as a whole has not received high level administrative support and impetus which it heeds and merits." This is from a May 5-8 report by the Senate Atomic Energy Committee (do not confuse with the A.E. Commission). We imagine by support the senators mean investigation? Well, Well, page George Van Tassel!

The good senators wound up in a tizzy, ruffled at not getting answers to radiation danger questions.

"The Committee called for less secrecy...." Shall we say, "We told you so!"?

The people who vomited en masse in Wyoming, Indiana and Ohio (A.P. Aug. 23 '59) may not be suffering from "food poisoning" but from radiation--the symptoms include vomiting, nausea and fever! Anyway officials running these typical American picnics deny being careless with the food except one group that left ham sandwiches in a truck in 93 degree temperature.

The doctors were puzzled in most cases. Are you?

N.Y.S.I.B., MEMBERSHIP, $4.00 per annum, payable

at the rate of $2.00 every six months, JANUARY,/ JUNE.
(includes U.F.O. MATION.)

UFO-mation

Published Quarterly by NYSIB: The New York Saucer Information Bureau

VOL. 1.   FALL ISSUE   NO. 4.

Published Quarterly by NYSIB: The New York Saucer Information Bureau

VOL. I. FALL ISSUE NO. 4.

1959 SUMMARY.

New Yorkers will assume that U.F.O. activity in or above our atmosphere is dead, if they depend upon our local news source for information.

The year 1959 was far from being inactive, however. On the West Coast, Gabe Green was vindicated in his prophecy. The Seven Sheriffs could hardly be discounted, as the seven dwarfs might be in <u>this</u> Snow-White story. Researchers are drawing blanks, and the press is not being of any help in fighting for, "freedom of the press." The U. P. I. apparently has a "Tomp" for any world news that might scare us!

The Weather Balloon over the East Coast on October 28, 1959, is a typical example of what happens to the uninformed mind. It panics. No one knew in advance, not even pilots flying commercial planes, or the U.S. Weather Bureau! It caused traffic jams, police officers to grab riot guns, and it frightened old ladies into believing the Russians were coming!

The Journal-American, on October 29, 1959, printed this head line: "Jitters and Balloon Soar in Space Test." This mediocre effort of ours only frightened our ignorant public. Another balloon developed by Arthur D. Little, Inc., will also cause us more confusion.

This column should be devoted to sightings, but we feel that the efforts made to suppress sightings or information about them is more important. Especially as N.Y.S.I.B. is a New York publication. Most of our information comes from outside the New York City area.

We must always remember that this small area houses about 11 million souls. They are at the mercy of the powers that be!

If you tend to think this writer is a bit fanatical on this subject, read this quote from the New York Journal-American; Bob Considine's column, "On the Line": "Basic lack of trust in the ability of a great people to "take it" is behind much of today's suppression of news, and that can only be suicidal to all of us in the long run!"

(Continued on page 57)

PUBLISHED BY

THE NEW YORK SAUCER INFORMATION BUREAU
P.O. Box 26 - Planetarium Station
New York 24, New York

THE STAFF:

Editor .... John Hay

Co-Editor .... Constance Lois Jessop

Gen. Assistant .... Lou Becker

Statements made in this publication are not the official expression of N.Y.S.I.B., or its Officers, unless stated to be an official communication.

EXCHANGE CO-OPERATIVES

Dr. Pauline Eastham,
9908 Pershing Drive,
EL PASO, TEXAS

Saucers Space & Science,
1157 St. Clair Ave., West,
TORONTO 10, ONT. CANADA

TRUFO, L. E. Lindwig,
4645 W. Adams Street,
CHICAGO 44, ILLINOIS

U.F.O. Research Bureau
R. R. 3, Danville,
INDIANA, INDIANA

U. F. O. SCHWEIX
Nadelberg 31,
BASEL, SWITZERLAND

SPAN. Jeanne S. Bagby,
521 East 87th Street
NEW YORK 28, NEW YORK

N.Y.S.I.B. OFFICERS

Director .... Bruce M. Dolen

Asst. Director &
Lecture Chairman .... Constance Lois Jessop

Secretary .... Ethel Goldenberg

Treasurer .... Lou Becker

Librarian .... Adrienne Munkeberg

Sgt. at Arms .... Hank Dannenberg

N.Y.S.I.B. MEMBERSHIP $4.00 per annum, payable at the rate of $2.00 every six months; JANUARY/JUNE. (includes UFOmation.)

THE EDITOR SPEAKS

Your Editor has been privileged to examine a great deal of the U.F.O. literature published in 1959, from all over the world. The archives of N.Y.S.I.B. will contain, when classified and catalogued, an extraordinary volume of material. This is because of N.Y.S.I.B.'s policy - friendly and tolerant to all U.F.O. organizations, no matter what their beliefs or aims. As a result, we receive samples of U.F.O. printed material that we believe others do not. We do not say this smugly, but only to point up the fact that N.Y.S.I.B.'s policy - your policy - is one that is universal in appeal; namely, brotherly love in action.

We feel it our duty to report in this issue our honest appraisal of this literature. It will naturally be personal and not an official N.Y.S.I.B. judgement, as many no doubt might disagree with the Editor's findings.

Only broad general observations can be made, as the literature is too vast, too wide-spread all over the world in all languages, to even attempt to do anything but classify. Every country seems to produce a type of literature that reflects its' current trend of thinking. However, each country reports the activities going on in other countries. Only in the U.S.A. does a curtain seem to fall down, and we get our "news" via the back door, as it were!

In Europe there seems, as in South America, to be a more intellectual approach to the subject. More professional men, that is to say, doctors, lawyers and engineers, take positions as officers in U.F.O. clubs, and the magazines are edited in a very much more impersonal way than in the U.S.A. From these "foreign" magazines we can glean the Russian attitude towards U.F.O.'s and the topic of space and space travel. The scientists in Russia apparently look forward to finding inhabited regions in space! Logic, not sentiment, dictates this conclusion. Another search seems to be for free energy. These two basic conclusions bring us sharply back into focus to the U.F.O. activity in the U.S.A. This is the message of the contact stories!

In the U.S.A. respectable professional people are either unaware of the situation or fear, because of censorship or ridicule to be connected with the type of U.F.O. organizations that exist here. In the U.S.A., the majority of U.F.O. groups are concerned with the psychic or occult aspect of the Flying Saucer phenonema. This is the only "way out", when we have so much security in the scientific area. Our administration wants to be sure the Russians don't learn how we circle the moon! The average American soberly realizes now that we are no longer leaders in atomic or missle development.

Continually we are told by the different agencies of the administration that U.F.O.'s don't exist except as mirages, hallucinations, and natural phenomenae - and on the other hand we read,

(continued on page 58)

SAUCER SCIENCE

By John Hay

What, actually, is a U.F.O.? It can be anything that is not nailed down, from a fast-moving mass of cosmic debris to a bit of energy as small as a molecule.

Each "expert" can classify, if the U.F.O. fits into the experience and knowledge of the observer. A simple cloud chamber any kid can build will reveal the mysterious cosmic rays. These are not classified as U.F.O.'s, even tho' the source or origin is a speculation!

But put a mass of them together, or any group of light particles under apparent intelligent control - and we have a U.F.O!! It becomes an object, solid or not, when it can be recorded by the eye, radar or the camera. For any image placed on film gets there only by focus. Out of focus, the image, although registering accurately and in proportion, seems, to our understanding, an unintelligible blur, a nothing!

Energy, or light particles in proper focus, seem to be solid objects; objectively they are; subjectively they are not .... but have a relative objectivity that exists as a sort of antimatter, or something within nothing. Under proper focus might these blurs of light be Space Ships, or something that can be a vehicle - for consciousness?

We are continually examining phenomenae with the obsolete rationale of the 20th Century. It is passé. So much is known that is kept hidden that the average man's thinking will never catch up, and as a result only new superstitions will grow, and a confused priestcraft of science will have to flounder in its own babel.

Einstein's conceptions - gleaned from Philosophy - are that matter is energy, energy is light, heat and motion, and that all space is in motion or rest (Yang and Yin) creating for us (within our scale of consciousness) light and dark. Only by light and dark can we distinguish anything, except for the one faculty of touch. Touch is life. Without this one sense, the persona gratia (I AM) loses contact with the material world, be it his own body or some external object.

This "unified field" theory has kicked the bottom out of our pail of collected facts. All are One. This psychological insecurity has created panic.

Professor Carl Jung admits a "puzzlement". Let us quote from "Flying Saucers a Modern Myth", page 149: "The simultaneous visual and radar sightings would, in themselves, be a satisfactory

(continued on page 59)

FOREIGN NEWS.

In 1961 the U.S. hopes to fire the rocket "Vegar" at Venus. General Dynamics Corp. holds the contract worth 33,500,000.00 tax dollars! ("Light" - Australia).

H.C. Dodd, B.Sc., in an article entitled "Driving Powers for U.F.O.", covers the Von Reichenbach theories, Keely's "apergy", and the "Bielfield-Brown" effect and the "Fohat" of the Venusians - all in the above Australian magazine - all for $1.00 per annum!

14,000 years ago Vega was the Pole Star, and in another 12,000 years it will hold the same position again. The reason for this is the fact that Vega lies on the circle which an imaginary continuation of the earth's axis sweeps out in the sky every 26,000 years.

Altair completes the Triangle. It is only 6 light-years distant, and only 10 times as bright as the sun. Like Deneb, it is of a fierce, white colour.

Each of these three stars has a faint companion, but in all three cases it is only that a faint star happens to be in the same line of sight as the main star, and none of them is a "double star" in the true sense of the word.

Between the Summer Triangle and the horizon lies the most interesting part of the "Milky Way". Here we find star clouds, which mark the centre of the Galactic System, of which our sun is but one of the smaller members, and we find also nebulae, star streams and "coal sacks", black patches in the sky, where cosmic dust blots out the light of the stars behind. The most striking of these dark nebulae is in the constellation Aquila. This is best seen with the aid of field-glasses, magnifying not more than 6 or 8 times. (Flying Saucer Review - Hon. B. le Poer Trench).

Irish Saucer Group. First steps towards the formation of an Irish flying saucer group are being taken by an enthusiast, Peter Gill. Will all those in Ireland who would like to join please write to Mr. Gill at Newtown Farm, Sandyford, County Dublin, Eire. (Flying Saucer Review - Hon. B. le Poer Trench).

Lord Dowding Lectures on Saucers. Air Chief Marshall Lord Dowding spoke recently to members of Salisbury Rotary Club in England, about flying saucers. He said the subject was a vast one and the existence of these craft was completely beyond doubt. He told his audience, "There have been literally hundreds of thousands of sightings observed by reputable people, including those in the Royal Observer Corps and pilots of aircraft."

He said that in the U.S.A., planes had gone in pursuit of the saucers, and in one case there had been a collision which had resulted in the total disintegration of the plane.

Radar operators had seen them on their screens. Lord Dowd-

(continued on page 60)

The U F O IN LITERATURE

Dr. Carl Jung's book, "Flying Saucers a Modern Myth", should be read and on the book shelf of every Saucer fan.

As far as we know no other Saucer book comes as close to the secret of the Saucers as does Prof. Jung's book. However, he does not press the issue too far; perhaps for personal reasons, or because of scientific or ethical reasons - along with the required, professional respect which is a must in the search for knowledge.

All of us must realize that a man may believe certain things personally and not be able to prove them, and at the same time, as a professional man, must reflect these same ideas professionally until proof has been established. Proof, of course, is a mechanical thing in America.

On page 4 of, "Saucers Space and Science", No. 12, October, 1959, we read about Willy Ley and his conclusions. They are convincing except for two dogmatic statements. One re ball lighting "...sea level air is too dense to permits it's formation". On Oc. 11, 1959, two such objects as Ley describes were seen over Larchmont, New York, so either they were not fire-balls, or fire-balls act very differently from Ley's knowledge of them.

Ley's story, "Space Visitors Held Possible", in the Montreal Star, January 4, 1958, winds up with, "I will be convinced, if I am shown wreckage, machinery or bodies". Well, yours truly could show him a cemetery and have a tough time convincing him that the "reality" that once activated these wreckages, or these obsolete machines, is invisible and is a mystery as much as the U.F.O.'s.

Without atacking Ley's idea too much, let us consider Worrell Keely's motor and the invisible force that activated it. Tuning forks any child can play with and the response "seems" miraculous - an invisible something moving an inanimate object. (maybe Gabriel's horn was supposed to raise the dead in such a manner?) Now if we consider sonar and its possibilities, we can easily imagine how it is possible for "poltergeisting" to happen! We can identify the objects that fly in the poltergeist (throwing ghost) phenomenae, but the means and methods are unknown. This is common in the U.F.O. story.

Dr. Nandor Fodor's book, "On the Trail of the Poltergeist", (Citadel Press) should be read for the mystery of "levitation", "apporting of material" objects- and such is the mystery of sex!! All contactees report both sexes aboard the contact saucers. (The robot saucers are different). The carrier beams of the Universal energy are men and women, as is electric phenomenae. "The souls, of men, are fire-balls" - page 133, "The Flying Saucers a Modern Myth", by Carl G. Jung.

In Fodor's book, page 9, paragraph 3, we read this strange admission, "..and also displayed his powers as a poltergeist, by making various articles in the room rattle on the furniture." And this is how Jung amazed his teacher, Dr. Freud!

1959 SUMMARY

(continued from page 51)

When Defense Secretary Neil McElroy has power to suppress a book ("Design for Survival", by Gen. Thomas E. Powers, Commander-in-Chief of the Strategic Air Command), no wonder the Air Force Association Magazine editorially states, "It has been made clear that the <u>Administration</u> disagrees sharply with General Powers' conviction that the public has become aware that military problems no longer are the, 'sole concern of men in uniform and the civilian superiors' ".

We, the public, may be confused about space, but not as much apparently, as those who are charged by vote with the responsibility of keeping us in TRUTH.

Your Editor, in the first issue of UFOmation, Volume 1, No 1, drew attention to this news suppression, and at this late date certain newspapermen are waking up like Rip Van Winkles!

In closing, let us state that we all now admit that we trail the Russians in space achievement, "as any fool can plainly see", but, more deadly is the fact that we trail them much more slowly in our <u>thinking</u> and philosophy about outer space. Perhaps we are strangled by fear or religious myopia.

From London (note: not Washington) AP, September 29, 1959 - "Earthlings to join Spacelings". The Soviet Scientist Feliks Segal says, "Consequently, there must be about 150,000 inhabited, planetary systems in our galaxy....some of them may even have begun to make flights into space. Therefore we should have meetings with them". He states <u>they</u> must be above and below us in development, and eventually meetings must take place! Sounds like Adamski or Williamson - at least <u>not</u> like our official Pontiff Menzel!

* * * * * * * * * * * *

MORE GOINGS ON OVER DURBAN!

At least four Durban people watched the unusual cavorting in the sky of a U.F.O. on June 4. One of them, a motorist, described the object as a silvery circular craft about 30 feet in diameter. It travelled slowly from the Stamford Hill area towards Umhlanga Rocks, where it swung out to sea. It was spotted at 11 AM. The motorist said he stopped his car and watched the UFO for about 10 minutes. Another motorist and two native women also watched. He said the UFO was "something fantastic". He was certain it was not an aircraft.

(Source: Natal Daily News, June 4 - Credit Langton Zank of Durban.) From: Flying Saucer Review.

* * * * * * * * * * * *

THE EDITOR SPEAKS   (continued from page 53)

Lord Dowding, head of the R.A.F. of Great Britain, has reportedly made the statement that he believes the U.F.O. are interplanetary - that the U.S.A. Airforce has aggressively tangled with the U.F.O's, and that we are desperately suppressing these facts!

Americans are appearing in print, in English-speaking U.F.O. magazines, deploring the "scene stealing" of the Amalgamated U.S. U.F.O. organizations - and they say our public won't give serious thought to the U.F.O.'s as long as "nuts" and the "lunatic fringe" take over. This type of orthodox thinking explains our "hidden caste" system and intellectual snobbery. If it persists we only will be the losers.

The U.F.O.'s will come and go as they have for centuries, regardless of our belief or unbelief. Sober Russian scientists are forced to believe an interplanetary vehicle exploded in 1908 - in Siberia. Official speculation is that it came from Venus. This was also a prophecy of American contactees. Interplanetary beings are embodied here for that purpose. The bright side of this report is that T.V. is gradually, through entertainment, bringing the message to the general public.

Our final comment, due to lack of space, is: Does censorship exist here? To answer that, let us quote from our press; Chicago Daily News Service headline, "Secrecy in Government Causes Added Worries on Capitol Hill". Being questioned, Ike "heatedly snapped", "Frankly, I don't believe it".

"A statement like this by the President will encourage further abuse" - Rep. John Moss (D.Calif). Perhaps it is better to just play golf!

* * * * * * * * * *

Green Space Ship over Ethiopia: A spherical-shaped, greenish object appeared at noon over Yergalem, the main town of Sidamo Province, in the south of Ethiopia. It flew with a swaying motion several times over the town. (Source: Mombasa Times, Kenya, April 18; Sunday News, Dar-es-Salaam, April 19.)

Flying Saucer over Chile: A mysterious object was seen by many people as it flew over the port of Ancud, Southern Chile, on June 1, at 8:00 p.m. for about 30 minutes. It moved noiselessly, sometimes at great speed, sometimes at low speed. Its colour changed from red to violet as it varied speed. Among the many witnesses were the occupants of a lorry belonging to the Office of Road Welfare of Chiloe (Province) and one of those on the vehicle was the Provincial Technical Officer, Enrique Saldivia. (Source: El Mercurio, Valparaiso, June 4; La Union, June 4).

From: Flying Saucer Review
1 Doughty Street
London W.C.1., England.

SAUCER SCIENCE (continued from page 54)

proof of their reality. Unfortunately, well authenticated reports show that there are also cases where the eye sees something that does not appear on the radar screen, or where an object undoubtedly picked up by radar is not seen by the eye".

Elsewhere in his book he elaborates upon the historical value of U.F.O.'s, and their connection with the sex drive. Oriental Mandalas are bi-sexual and the most commonly known is the Yang and Yin Symbol. When activated, it is a vortex or spiral motion, as witnessed in outer space in the creation of a nebulae, a star, or planet.

The mystery is that these "unsolid visions" of light seem to be under an intelligent control or direction, or are intelligent themselves!

Philosophy is, perhaps, America's most neglected study. The Gold Rush takes so much time. Any philosopher will admit that behind any creation is a Thinker - be it man, or nature's form and, formless, energy.

Man creates objects that **all** come out of space, be it a TV set or a mouse-trap. The Unknown that all religions designate a God creates from the mystery of space.

The latest hassel is to try and stop the idea that SPACE and religion have anything in common. Out of space and time came man - out of time and space the **idea** of God. Out of space and time - come **ALL** material objects. Back into space goes ALL ... in time!

Man as a positive masculine unit seems to be always accompanied by the opposite, negative feminine polarity. It is the only way, so far, that he knows to recreate and perpetuate himself. It is not strange then, that all contact stories tell of women being aboard the Spacecraft.

* * * * * * * *

NEW EXCHANGE CO-OPERATIVES

Herbert Clark,
V.A.F.S.C.,
Box 720, Station A,
Vancouver, B.C., Canada

The Hon. Brinsley le Poer Trench
Flying Saucer Review
1 Doughty Street
London, W.C.1., England

* * * * * * * *

Dr. Harlow Shapley, former director, Harvard Observatory: "..... we must now accept it as inevitable...there are other worlds with thinking beings."

* * * * * * * *

FOREIGN NEWS   (continued from page 55)

ing said in conclusion, "Sooner or later these people will make a determined effort to contact people on this earth." (Flying Saucer Review - Hon. B. le Poer Trench).

Behind the Iron Curtain .... Saucer Group in Poland! Flying Saucer Review is now in touch with Kazimierz Zaleski in Warsaw. He is President of the Polish section of Association Mondialiste Interplanetaire. This is the international organization directed by Professor Alfred Nahon from Ferney-Voltaire (Ain-FRANCE). Professor Nahon edits the excellent newspaper "Le Courrier Interplanetaire" (in French).

Mr. Zaleski wishes to inform the world that his country is very interested in the U.F.O. question, and that he would like to get in touch with other saucer groups. His address is Warszawa 97, Post Box No. 1, Poland. Mr. Zaleski reports that two flying saucer lectures in his country recently have attracted large audiences and a number of others are scheduled to take place in the future. (Flying Saucer Review - Hon. B. le Poer Trench).

MAIL BAG - (Flying Saucer Review -- Hon. B. le Poer Trench).
Can They Hear our Thoughts?:

Sir:

On the hot afternoon of June 12, 1959, travelling by train along the east coast of India I rested my head for a moment on the window bars. My eyes closed and mentally I saw quite clearly one whom I knew to be a comrade from outer space. I mentally embraced him with feelings of affection and comradeship, saying mentally, "Brother"!

About eight hours later, on the high terrace of a friend's house in Kakinada, my friend N.V. Ramanamurti and I both saw very clearly two bright lights moving side by side from south-west to south-east at a rapid rate. As they approached the horizon they were seen clearly as domed discs, swaying to and from sideways, as though to let us see that they were really 'flying saucers'. We both had excellent views of them from several angles before they vanished, perhaps behind a row of tall trees. At first they were high up, but at the end not more than 1,000 ft., they shone with a faint white luminescence, were quite soundless and threw off neither sparks nor trails behind them.

The loss of sleep was compensated for by this blissful experience after so many years of desiring to see for oneself at least the vehicles used by these unknown friends of ours from other worlds. It seemed to both of us a definite reply to the wordless greeting sent out some hours before.

                              Duncan Greenlees,
                              Bhimunipatnam, Vizag. Dt.,
                              South India
                                        (continued on page 11).

FOREIGN NEWS (continued from page 60)

Americans who live "over the border", even though they speak American-English, and some of them have ancestors who settled in the Colonies that are now the United States, are considered foreigners, so we include some Canadian News Items under this section.

"Saucers Space and Science", c/o Gene Duplantier, 125 Woodycrest Avenue, Toronto 6, Ontario, Canada, publishes the fact that the "Kaizuka photos" originally published by the Mar.-Apr., 1959, Japan U. F. O. Intelligence Magazine, are fakes. This was first suspected by Dr. Fujinami, of Kyoto. To shorten the story, Yoshihiro Baba, the schoolboy, confessed he faked the pictures on an "innocent impulse" and that he "bears no malice"!

Integrity is so hard to find, except in professional people who love their art so as not to prostitute it. As we wrote in the last issue about Marcus Aurelius' thoughts on this subject, we cannot but point up again that Wisdom is timeless. Any good - and we mean good - craftsman could fake U.F.O. pictures and they would not be suspect.

The motive and honesty of the individual is the **only** guarantee we have of finding TRUTH.

From Queensland, Australia, the Magazine, "Light", a U.F.O. magazine edited from 20 Crawford Avenue, Stafford, Brisbane, Queensland, Australia, ($1.00 per annum) is excellent.

A report shows that out of ten lectures on Flying Saucers, the one with the largest attendence happens to be the one given before the "University Squadron R.A.A.F." Strange that Royal Airforce Pilots with University educations should be interested in such claptrap?

From Australia we read of the sad state of our Radar Traffic Control Systems around Washington. This is explained in "The UFO Enigma", by Keith Flitcroft (not flit-craft!) in the June, 1959, issue of the above magazine.

Danish Saucers are Squares (Copenhagen, February 25th). Two Scandinavian Airlines Pilots reported independently today that they had seen "square" flying saucers last night - over Denmark. (Light - Australia.)

Radio Moscow said, on January 21st, that the Soviet Union is working on a jet plane engine to be fueled with the inexhaustable electrically charged gas of the ionosphere, some 60 miles above earth. (Light - Australia).

We read somewhere that the British have already flown twice the speed of sound in an electric jet. - Ed.

www.ingramcontent.com/pod-product-compliance
Lightning Source LLC
Chambersburg PA
CBHW080255170426
43192CB00014BA/2672